THE NFT HANDBOOK

2 Books in 1 - The Complete Guide for Beginners and Intermediate to Start Your Online Business with Non-Fungible Tokens using Digital and Physical Art

Copyright © 2022

Clark Griffin

1 Table of Contents

2   AUTHOR'S NOTE

Crypto art AI is a team of cryptocurrency and art world enthusiasts that aim to spread the answers to common doubts about cryptocurrency and art world, directly and effectively.

3 INTRODUCTION

In creating Bitcoin, the idea of trustless, digital scarcity has been established. The fact that digital copies were too costly before the inception of the technology was a barrier to widespread use.

Because of the introduction of blockchain technology, it is now feasible to create programmable digital scarcity. This technology is now being utilized for the aim of linking the digital world with the physical world. Non fungible tokens are the first type of digital assets that is playable (NFTs). This may serve as a catapult to enhance digital products scarcity.

ERC-721 tokens cannot be easily interchangeable, which means they may be used to represent unique assets and proposals. In other words, tangible assets like real estate, artwork, and antiques may be represented precisely using this model.

The collectibles market is now valued at $450 billion and has stayed mostly unaltered since the internet took off. Current authentication problems, fraud, and monetary restrictions are commonplace in the business. At this point in time, the market is ready for a shift since blockchain technology can provide trustless transactions to a whole new level.

Real-life assets may be tokenized using NFTs, which offer a trustworthy and trustless method to do so.

The majority of the NFT market was constructed around Ethereum. With all the extra activity on EOS, people have started to show more interest. In line with this, it's no surprise that NFTs (non-fungible tokens) are appearing on new blockchains thanks to investment fueling development.

Non-fungible tokens (NFTs) are digital assets having distinct characteristics. A particular asset may have any number of different NFTs (e.g., one piece of art or one piece of real estate).

With these distinct qualities, the object's digital representation may be created. Real-world physical assets may be represented using NFTs. In a trustless setting, a distributed, community-owned ledger may store a representation and exchange it with others without the requirement for a centralized authority.

NFTs are one of the primary pillars of the emerging digital asset class - assets that have been digitized and have their own cryptocurrency token associated with them. We will go through the many features of NFTs, and how they are linked to other asset types.

These subjects will be covered in this book:

NFTs are polyhedral tessellations. As previously mentioned, there are various kinds and characteristics of NFTs.

Tokens of different kinds (fungible vs non-fungible) (NFTs).

An introduction to NFTs and noteworthy projects that use NFTs.

Legal and ethical concerns that are associated with the development of NFTs. Where to find and keep them.

Additional issues relating to NFTs include: How NFTs connect to photography, music, and video makers.

Additionally, we will also address some of the most frequent questions surrounding NFTs and their solutions.

To find out how to make your first NFT utilizing the Ethereum platform and some other platforms, we shall examine how to do this in more detail later. We will then discuss the role of NFTs in the market.

This book will explain the following topics:

What are NFTs? The different types and features of NFTs.

Difference between fungible and non-fungible tokens (NFTs).

The use cases for NFTs, and popular projects that use NFTs.

Ethical and legal issues around the creation of NFTs. How to acquire and store them.

We'll also cover other important topics related to NFTs, such as:

The relationship between NFTs and Photography, NFTs and Video Maker, NFTs and Musicians and DJ.

We will also discuss some common questions on NFTs and their answers.

Later, we will go over how to create your first NFT using the Ethereum platform and some other platforms. We'll then talk about NFTs market's place.

4 NON-FUNGIBLE TOKEN - MEANING

NFTs is an abbreviation for Non-Fungible Tokens; they are Cryptocurrency assets that act as a rare and unique project, whether virtual or physical, for example digital art or real estate. NFTs are as unique as a true pieces of art. A blockchain technology is used to recognize their authenticity so one will be able to tell the difference between a replica and original. This made it certified to be data carriers that act as the digital representation of a real-world asset, and it is used to represent physical assets, such as real estate, artwork, collectibles, and more. Digital assets like these have been touted as the next step for the global economy. They allow a real-world asset to be securely stored and transferred on the blockchain. Any item or artwork can be traced to the person who published it. This can be used to avoid fraud and manipulation that is prevalent in many markets today. Two of most famous types of NFTs are Cryptototties and Cryptopunks.

NFTs are a unique digital asset. To be more specific, they are the first major digital asset class to have been tokenized on the

5

blockchain. Since these assets do not conform to the fungible properties of traditional digital assets, we refer to them as non-fungible tokens. The term non-fungible is used because it implies that NFTs cannot be altered or duplicated without altering the value of the real-world asset being represented by them.

Through this feature, NFT offers buyers with ownership certificates of digital items and protects the value of their upcoming transactions. A CoinDesk report claims that artists can digitally sell their artwork to a globally that can generate higher profits at one-piece works and royalty plans. NFTs are a major upgrade over previous types of tokens.

Gamers can also own in-game property or goods and sell them to earn money. Most of the NFT tokens are manufactures using the two Ethereum standards ERC-1155 and ERC-721.

Cryptokitties, as a proof of concept, showed us that NFTs could represent digital collectibles. While this is a minor use case, it has proven that NFTs are something very new and unique. They have provided us with the foundations for bringing scarcity and digital ownership to a whole new level.

However, the increased activity on EOS has caused interest to shift. With investment driving the growth of the blockchain, it is no surprise that NFTs are also starting to appear on new blockchains. NFTs are still very new, and there have only been a few major uses for them so far. However, there is a lot of potential for various applications of NFTs in the future. The rise of digital asset exchanges will bring a new type of liquidity that was not possible before. The current state of the NFT market is very similar to what the cryptocurrency industry was like in its early days.

There are still many issues with how NFTs are defined and classified. There is also no agreed-upon standard for their creation and storage. The NFT market is still very much experimental in nature, but it has already managed to prove its usefulness in niche markets. It will take some time before this technology can be implemented on different applications, but this does not mean that it will not eventually get there. All of these potential uses will require a solution to the problem of NFT interoperability.

Real-world assets are not owned by anyone. The real-world assets that NFTs represent can only be owned by people who are registered as its owner on a blockchain. NFTs can only be properly owned and managed if their value is transferable on the blockchain. As with any other type of asset, a real-world asset's value can only be transferred if it has liquidity. Most people are already very familiar with the idea of owning digital items such as in-game assets, tickets, music albums, and others. The success that NFTs have had so far in these types of markets means that there will only be more adoption going forward.

As the public becomes more accustomed to using cryptocurrency exchange platforms, the demand for NFTs will also rise. It is often said that blockchain technology will disrupt a lot of industries. However, the industry where this could happen first would be online gaming. If NFTs can become useable on the blockchain, the opportunities they will create for games will be enormous.

The use of NFTs in games has already started to happen. There are already a number of game developers that are using NFTs for in-game assets. They have made these NFTs available for gamers to use in their favorite games. The ownership of these assets is managed on the blockchain, and this adds to their mainstream adoption. NFTs are not just limited to within games either. There are NFTs that can be used for other purposes outside of the gaming industry. NFTs can be used for in-app purchases or even as collectibles.

4.1 What is NFTs

Like physical money, Cryptocurrency is just like physical money, i.e., it is fungible. In other words, it can be used for buying or selling things, or for exchange from one currency to another. For example, the value of one bitcoin will always be equal to another Bitcoin. Same is the case for the ether. In digital economy, cryptocurrency is considered as secure transaction medium because of its fungibility.

NFTs change the crypto paradigm by making each token one-of-a-kind and irreplaceable, making them non-fungible, meaning that one token may be worth more than the others. Due to distinct and non-transferable ID , digital asset representations are equated with digital passports to differentiate it from other tokens. There is the possibility of expansion. In other words two NFT's can "breed" to form the the third, unique NFFT.

NFTs, similar to the Bitcoin, contain detailed ownership to make the process of verification and exchange of token between the holders a lot easier. There is the possibility for the owners to add asset-related metadata or attributes in the NFT. For example, Coffee beans taken as token can be included fair trade category. Alternatively, artists can use their own metadata signature to sign their digital artwork.

ERC-721 standard was used to develop NFTs, by the same person who manages the ERC-20 Intelligent Contract. The ERC-721 is used to defines the minimum interface that is needed for trading of game tokens. The interface includes property information, safety, and metadata. The ERC-1155 standard is defined as decreasing the transaction and storage costs in single contract as necessary needed for NFTs and batch in various non-fungible tokens.

In November 2017, the most famous incident occurs in history of NFT, i.e., the release of Cryptokitties. Cryptokitties are represented as a digital cat with an EthereumBlockchain unique ID. Each kitten is distinct and its trade occurs in Ether. They breed with each other and form new descendants with attributes and assessments that are different from their parents. Cryptokitties, after its launch, in no time, accumulated a fan base that actively purchased, exchanged and distributed ether and spent $ 20 million. Some fans goes far in their efforts to the point that they even went from $ 100,000.

Although the Cryptokitties' is considered not so important but it has significant commercial applications. For example, NFTs have been used at real estate level and also for personal transactions. The benefit of allowing different type of tokens in contract increases trust on these tokens, whether they are used for real estate or for single transactions.

4.2   Fungibility in NFTs

The capacity of an asset to be exchanged for a similar item without losing its value is referred to as fungibility. The properties of an asset, such as divisibility and value, are also defined by fungibility.

For example, the value of two $ 10 bill, when compared, remains the same. For example, when you lend a $ 10 bill, you can return it in the form of another type that has the same value as of this $10 bill, instead of returning the same note.

In the world of digital currency, the value of one BTC us similar to that of the other one. But same is not the case for non-fungible tokens. In this case, the value of the NFT token will be different from similar token. Each token has its own unique characteristics and the assets of the real world, such as the rare stones, artworks and the luxury products of the collector.

4.3 Fungible and non-fungible

Fungible tokens are tokens whose value remains same on exchange. As discussed previously, the value of Bitcoin is not dependent on its owner or history and remains the same. That's why it is known as fungible token.

However, a non-fungible token are distinct from one another and trade cannot be occur in another form. As discussed about bitcoin earlier, but on the other hand, a non-fungible token is one of unique trading card. You can get something else if you exchange it with completely different card.

4.4 Characteristics of NFTs

Rarity: Rarity defines the value of the NFT. Thus, desired amount of tokens can be developed by NFT developers and to increase its value, they sometimes restricts the development of these tokens.

Insaperable: NFTs are inseparable. They cannot be broken down to smaller units. You can either purchase the entire a piece of digital art, or does not buy any art.

Unique: it is the most important characteristic among all. They register themselves as unique in a permanent information tab. They consider these features as originality certificate.

Whether it is a GIF or an image, creating your own NFT artwork is an easy process and requires less or no knowledge about cryptocurrency. NFT can be utilized in developing collectibles and also stacks of digital cards. Since the art is generated from the blockchain, it's possible to use an image created on one chain and transfer it over to another.

NFTs can be created with any digital art creation software, such as Photoshop or The Gimp. You'll also need to convert your image into an ASCII art file for it to be readable by Etheremon or similar games. Some digital art creation software such as Gimp provides the option to encode the file into base64 or an image format that can be read by Etheremon.

Creating an NFT usually entails taking your piece of digital art and encoding it in a compatible image format. If you're not familiar with how to do this, you may want to use Gimp to encode your digital art into a compatible file type. The final step is to transfer the file to the blockchain and register it with an address.

What is the cost of making an NFTs? Thankfully, there are currently a number of tools that allow you to create NFTs for free! Some of the tools include Etheremon, CryptoKitties, and CryptoPunks. You can also use digital art creation software such as Gimp.

One of the biggest hurdles is creating an account for your NFT. Since it's a digital asset, you'll need to register with a blockchain wallet service provider, such as MyEtherWallet or MetaMask.

Developers can use open-source tools such as the ERC-721 to create and manage the NFTs on the Ethereum blockchain. There are also a number of third-party applications that developers can use to create and manage NFTs. Some of these include Ethers.JS.

NFTs are not limited to being in games; however, they can also be used for other purposes outside of gaming. Some of the uses of NFTs outside of gaming include:

- Art Industry: This allows artists to sell their digital work.

- Real Estate: Digital real estate and 3D assets like furniture can be easily transact using NFT.

- Musicians: Selling the rights and originals of their work and short video clips of their music.

There are so many ways that NFTs can be used in games, and this is what makes them so exciting for game developers. Some of the limitations that developers face with NFTs include the size and complexity that they can have on games. As more developers discover these possibilities, NFTs are starting to look like a viable option.

An NFT is a new technology in the gaming world that can create very powerful and flexible virtual items and experiences. They can do this by applying an Ethereum smart contract to a virtual item, allowing the item to be distributed ("leased") between two parties without ever having to touch it or interact with it. These types of contracts are useful in games and other industries as well.

In the real estate industry, a seller may not want to spend time and money finding a buyer for a property, but instead, the seller can "lease" its listing to another real estate agent for a fixed fee. A contract can be drawn up that describes how the virtual property will be used and what will happen if the cause of action arises. The contract can also contain guidelines that describe how items in this virtual world must behave according to the specified design specifications.

Non-fungible tokens are more like digital assets than digital currencies. In order to transfer an asset from one party to another, the asset must be unique. These types of tokens are not interchangeable or divisible, as this would cause their value to change due to changes in supply and demand.

The NFTs can be utilized for a wide array of reasons. Some of these include:

NFTs are very rare and unique. If you combine NFTs with digital identities, then you can create operable real-world assets on the blockchain. Traditional digital items that we know today lack ownership and scarcity, so they cannot be considered real-world assets. Since NFTs are implemented with smart contracts, this allows them to have fungible digital identities, which means that they can also act as real-world assets.

NFTs can be used to facilitate smart contracts. They can be used to manage the digital assets on the blockchain. This means that they can also manage things like escrows, in-game assets, and more. Not only are they able to perform these tasks, but they can also offer a new level of complexity. The increase in complexity has many positive outcomes for all stakeholders involved:

Another use case is related to exchanging digital assets for real-world ones using NFTs as the medium of exchange. This scenario is more popular in the gaming industry than in other industries, but the idea of exchanging digital items for real-world ones is not limited to that.

In the gaming industry, a user can buy digital items within the game using NFTs. This gives them increased flexibility and control over their assets as they can access their NFTs from anywhere. Since these virtual assets are stored on the blockchain, they are much safer and notable than traditional digital items. This means that there is less risk of fraud and scams when dealing with NFTs. If a player wants to trade their digital items, they can easily do so outside of the game using NFTs as the medium of exchange. A user's profile is not only their in-game credentials and scores but also includes a collection of their digital assets. This allows them to maintain full control over these assets while still being able to use them in the most convenient way possible. An example of this can be seen in the game, CryptoKitties. CryptoKitties is an online game that specializes in collecting digital collectibles. It allows users to purchase and collect kitties, which can be traded and sold – just like traditional digital items.

The player who purchases any CryptoKitties collects virtual assets that are stored on the blockchain. These virtual assets are unique and are controlled by the player only. This means that there is no risk of being scammed or losing access to them.

4.5 The Future of Art Market in the Blockchain industry

If the visionaries have their way, NFTs, blockchain, and ethers will stand out in future art market. If the skeptics have what they want, then the future hype will make art too expensive compared to a work of art that is too bad.

Mike Winkelmann, pseudonym Beeple, from the United States, has been releasing a piece every day for almost 13 years without skipping a single day. On Instagram, he has 1.8 million followers but no gallery. Justin Bieber wore his artwork during shows, and Louis Vuitton reproduced it on clothing. He is also a father and a graphic designer. And it's clear that art has been something he's done in the past because he's done it. And art has definitely been something for him that he has done in the past because he has choose this for himself. He states on his website, "He's dabbling in a wide range of artistic endeavors. Some of it is good, but a lot of it is very bad. Every day, he's striving to make it less crap, so bear with him).".

On December of the last year, On Nifty Gateway, which is considered as a digital art marketplace. There, he established an auction, when he earned almost $ 3.5 million for 20 of his paintings. Now at Christie's, it's collage of about 5,000 pieces daily, it's been heard by experts that it sells for minimum of $ 50 million, and it's still underrated.

4.6 Hype for art

"'Beeple Mania': How Mike Winkelmann Makes Millions sold Pixels" was few days ago, the headline of "Esquire". Furthermore, cat madness surrounds along with Beeple-Mania. "Why an Animation Flying Cat with a Pop-Tart Body selling for Almost $ 600,000, " on Monday, becomes the headline of the New York Times. Art market has everything. The price of each piece of art is very high and media are turning over. Only at this moment, things aren't seem to be similar as they've always been, since digital art is now being sold for which there was previously no market. Although, in addition to the fact that almost anybody in the art world has noticed, it's already disappearing like hotcakes on the markets. There are famous various art marketplace that includes Nifty Gateway, Foundation, Rarible, SuperRare, MakersPlace, Zora, and KnownOrigin.

All of this necessitates a great deal of debate. What's the big deal about this? Why do people purchase digital art in the first place? What are your plans for it? What role do NFTs play in all of this? And what exactly are NFTs? Clubhouse, an audio-based social network, is presently satiating the demand for information and interaction. The application is trying to explain the importance of NFTs in future for several weeks.

While sitting in the room, I offen heared the statement "NFTs and the Future of the Art" and I hear it from time to time. People constantly talk about destruction and democratization of cryptocurrency, crypto wallet, drops and tokens which includes Ethereum, BTC, Nifty and SuperRare.

Those who know their way are sometimes getting new information and new ideas. you'll be embarrassed and angry and leave the room immediately, If you know nothing about NFT. Suppose an artist sells digital art for $ 1.4 million in five minutes. You cannot be able to understand certain quantities, if you are not aware of marketplace drop culture.

4.7 Key function

NFTs are sophisticated forms of basic encryption. The contemporary financial system comprises of sophisticated trading and lending systems for many kinds of assets, from immovable to loan and artworks. NFTs are in the process of redesigning this infrastructure by allowing digital physical asset representation. To make sure the idea of digital physical asset demarcation is nothing new and does not require separate identification. Although these ideas coupled with the benefits of size-resistant intelligent contract blockchain may become a strong force for change.

Maybe the efficiency of the market helps NFT directly. Converting tangible advantages into digital works may remove middlemen and make the procedure simple. NFTs in block diagrams that depict real or digital drawings remove the need for agencies and enable artists to connect directly with the audience. They may also enhance their processes for businesses. For instance, the NFT of a bottle of wine will facilitate the connection and controlling of the source, manufacture and sales of each participant in the supply chain. Ernst & Young has created a customer solution.

Non-fermentable tokens are also extremely good for the maintenance of identities. Consider where a physical passport must be submitted at all points of entrance and departure. Each passport has its own unique identifying features by transforming individual passports into NFTs, which may ease the procedure to enter and leave countries. In order to extend this use case, NFT may also be utilized in the digital world for identity management.

NFT may offer a new investment concept by dividing them into various amounts of tangible assets, such as property. A digital real estate asset is more simpler to divide into numerous owners than in real life. This tokenization ethic does not have to be confined to property. It may easily be extended to other materials like images. So an artwork doesn't require a single owner. Many owners may have a digital equivalent and each owner is accountable for portion of the diagram. These contracts may enhance their value and earnings.

New kinds of investing and markets are the interesting potential of NFTs.

4.8　Benefit of NFT

Non-fungible tokens opens a new dimension to digital world. Major advantages of NFTs are:

NFT are transferable unlike the exchangeable tokens on commercial markets. It is bought or sold on the NFT special market. But its value depends on itself.

They are real - the technological power of blockchain is an NFT token. Therefore, you know that your NFT is real, because it is almost impossible to use a decentralized and immutable master book to create forgeries.

They hold property rights. This also refers to the use of a decentralized NFT platform, the owner cannot change the data once committed.

- Please review my book here:
  http://www.amazon.com/review/create-review?&asin=B095M47KH4

- At the following link, you can access a **completely free online course** on "NFT Artist":

https://dl.bookfunnel.com/j699cthbam

5 ASSET FOR COLLECTIBLES

5.1 Main characteristics

The fungibility feature has been introduced in the previous chapter, but let's dive more into understanding what fungible assets mean. Fungible assets are assets that can be exchanged for other units of such assets. For example, one Bitcoin is the same as any other Bitcoin in circulation, similar to the Ether, Dollar and Euro. These are also divisible. In other words, they can be split into smaller pieces of units of the same asset. These assets are basically indistinguishable. This property is important to enable all assets to be run by payment method. In contrast, non-fungible tokens are cryptographic tokens that are uniquely indivisible. NFTs are based on contracts like ETH and DAI, but the contract also contains vital data that makes each NFT unique to the next NFT. As such, one NFT cannot be exchanged for another. It is not possible to break down one entire NFT into smaller units and use it. These properties indicate irreplaceability.

The idea of NFTs has been around since 2014, but it wasn't until 2017 that the first ERC-721 token was created. Since then, a handful of games have created their own NFTs to use as in-game items. The most popular example is CryptoKitties, which went viral in late 2017 primarily due to each kitty's unique nature and the ability to breed them and create new variations. Although that game is popular, NFTs aren't limited to just the games industry; other industries are starting to see the possibilities that NFTs provide.

The most popular use case for NFTs at the moment is in the gaming industry. Game developers have been using open-source tools such as ERC-721 to create NFTs on the Ethereum blockchain since 2016. However, 2018 has marked a rise in mainstream interest in these types of tokens.

As one of the first developer communities with a large number of active users, the gaming community was a driving force for NFTs in 2018. The idea of playing virtual items such as digital collectibles that can be traded and sold has already proven to be popular because of CryptoKitties.

However, NFTs are more than just a new form of in-game items. Multiple industries have found that NFTs can provide tremendous benefits to their business models.

This is because these virtual items are registered on the blockchain and can be managed and transferred in a secure manner. The main use case for NFTs outside the gaming industry is to create digital assets that will be used as a medium of exchange in other industries. The primary use for NFTs in these industries lies in the possibility of creating real-world assets using smart contracts. NFTs can be used to provide digital ownerships to real-world items through smart contracts. This means that one can trade their digital assets for physical assets outside of the virtual world without relying on a third party or middleman.

The gaming industry also has an interest in moving physical items out of blockchain and onto its network. This is because it would allow them to reduce costs and increase efficiency. For example, a high-quality game may have an inventory of tens of thousands of items. These items can be distributed by using NFTs and "leasing" them to users through smart contracts. The users can then associate their progress with those virtual items and purchase them in the future.

The most common concern surrounding NFTs is that they could be imbalanced in the future. This is because they can potentially provide any player with the same level of value and status. This means that a newbie player and a veteran player may have the same amount of value to the game. There are some ways to avoid this issue, though.

5.2 Complementary features

NFTs have proven to be a rare asset. Every token contains a code that indicates that it is the only asset with a unique digital ID. It is useful for generating your own digital assets and can also be used for representing rare assets (physical assets) whose tree of ownership can be traced. The possibilities for rare and exclusive items to trade, including game pieces nad digital art collectibles, are endless. Platforms such as Nifty Gateway, Open Sea, and Rarible provide NFTs with an increasing consumer base.

The use cases of NFT are as follows:

- Create digital or crypto collectibles.

- Proving authenticity of digital art, and at the same time allowing artists to retain their copyright and IP

- Management of digital items ownership within blockchain-integrated games

- Allows ownership of parts of expensive items such as real estate.

- Devised a digital ID system that enables users control information by staying at one plance.

A famous application for NFTs to date is CryptoKitties, an Ethereum- based game that allows for the buying, selling digital cats including their breeding. CryptoKitties was released on November 28, 2017 and recorded $ 15 million in transactions with more than 150,000 users for the first time in two weeks. One of the CryptoKitties, sold for $ 170,000, has created a viral sensation that has drawn the platform to Etherium and worldwide interest.

The success of CryptoKitties has caused severe transaction congestion on the Ethereum network. The result is encouraging the adoption of CryptoKitties in the press with a lot of money that is scrambled to counter the network's negotiability, and also exchanged for digital cats. This has resulted in great recognition for blockchain as an innovative tech that offers more than just a cryptocurrency.

6 HISTORY OF NON-FUNGIBLE TOKENS

Let's delve into the history of what non-fungible tokens are, where we understand their functions and uses, and deepen our understanding of how they are being used in trade. Non-fungible tokens have been around since the beginning of blockchain technology. The first cryptocurrency ever launched, Bitcoin, created a digital asset that was completely controlled by its developers. These assets were referred to as "bitcoins," and they gave their owners a certain level of value. The coins could be owned by a user and used to purchase or sell real-world assets (mainly BTC) through the Bitcoin network. This meant that these assets could be used to create fiat money on the blockchain, which was unprecedented at the time. This gave Bitcoin early adopters an edge over others who were looking to purchase cryptocurrencies because there was a clear way of using them to purchase real-world goods. Some of the first NFT games were created with Bitcoin in mind. For instance, Spells of Genesis (SoG) and CryptoKitties both make it possible for users to spend their cryptocurrencies in a game.

The popularity of NFTs began to grow significantly in 2017 and 2018. This was mainly because of the increased attention and usage of cryptocurrencies on the blockchain. Up until this point, games using blockchain technology were mainly focused on creating a digital asset that could be exchanged for real-world assets (fiat). However, more and more users were becoming interested in using NFTs and other blockchain tools to create advanced game experiences. This resulted in the creation of CryptoKitties, which became an instant success. By the end of 2017, it received more than $12 million in funds from investors. This was huge at the time, especially for a blockchain-based game. The price of a CryptoKitty was reportedly so high that a digital cat went for $110,000. This means that it was on par with the price of a work of art! This shows just how valuable NFTs can be. They can be used to create assets that have real-world value, not just game value. It was after the success of CryptoKitties that the ERC-721 standard was created. One of the main reasons this standard came about is because of CryptoKitties and the fact that it introduced NFTs to an even larger audience. This meant that people who had never heard about blockchain technology previously now understood what they were, how they worked, and how they could be used in a game. Around this time, blockchain technology started to become more mainstream, which also helped increase the number of developers who saw value in NFTs and other blockchain tools.

Today, non-fungible tokens can be used by any game because they are easy to build and integrate. The popularity of NFTs has led to many other possibilities for games that were previously thought impossible. It's also worth noting that many games are now designed to increase the value of NFTs. This is because, as we discussed earlier, NFTs are more valuable and can have more functions than standard digital assets. For example, CryptoKitties tracks the total number of cats that have been created and even allows users to collect and trade them.

In the near future, we will start to see a lot of games that use non-fungible tokens as their core currency. This will allow players to use NFTs to purchase items, services, and other assets within the game. These assets can be of any kind, including weapons and vehicles.

6.1   Non-Fungible Tokens Myths

There are several myths surrounding NFTs and non-fungible tokens. This is understandable, considering that most of these myths have been around for years. Here's a list of some of the more common myths:

1) Myth: "Ethereum has thousands of pending transactions" – This is one of the most common misconceptions about Ethereum. It reveals a misunderstanding about how blockchains work and how they process data. In fact, the amount of pending transactions has nothing to do with the number of people using the network or its popularity. It simply means that there are many pending transactions in this block, which is actually a good thing because it means that many developers and users are using Ethereum. The more people who use Ethereum, the more valuable it becomes.

2) Myth: "NFTs are a scam" – This is another common misconception about NFTs. This is true in some markets, but it is not the case in most cases. A few years ago, this was true because people were unfamiliar with the concept of non-fungible tokens. However, as time went on and more people

understood what they were, this myth died out. Today, many professional traders who understand NFTs and blockchain technology's benefits are starting to view them as an investment rather than a scam.

This was shown by the fact that nine percent of all NFTs were traded on the Ethereum network during 2018.

3) Myth: "NFTs are too volatile" – This is another common misconception about non-fungible tokens. The price of an NFT will go up and down, just like any other coin or token. This is because it is not linked to a specific item and can be used in any number of games. That is why it can be traded for items in games as well as real-world assets.

4) Myth: "NFTs are too expensive" – This is not true at all. The price of NFTs varies, but the average cost is equivalent to that of other cryptocurrencies, which are already cheap compared to traditional currencies. This means you can get as many NFTs as you want for a fraction of the cost of a traditional currency.

5) Myth: "NFTs are too complicated and hard to create" – This is not true, either. It all depends on the game developer and which blockchain platform they are using. Since there are so many different types of blockchain platforms, developers will be able to use whichever one they prefer. However, if they are

using Ethereum, they can use NFT-Crowdfund to create their own NFT token. This means they can rely on a protocol to create their NFT without learning a new programming language or building their own smart contracts. The only thing they will need is some knowledge about Ethereum and how it works.

6) Myth: "NFTs don't bring value to the gaming industry" – This is another common misconception about non-fungible tokens. There are a lot of games that allow you to collect NFTs. This means that these features can increase the value of an NFT. After all, NFTs can be used in many different forms, including virtual items in games such as CryptoKitties and Spells of Genesis.

6.2 Problems or Controversies

When you tear off the first layer of NFTs, some overlapping issues start to arise which are: environmental, logistical, ethical, etc.

Many have pointed out the impact (extreme ecological impact) of NFT formation and trade explosions on planets already destroyed by climate change (climate change-related disasters, environment, racism, inequality). What is the relationship between NFTs and climate change? Simply put, a lot of energy is used along with the process of issuing NFTs, adding tokens to the blockchain and and the wave of transactions (bidding, resale, etc.). Multiplying that by a huge market driven by greed, we are initiating new forms of environmental destruction. Ethereum is a platform that hosts a fixed blockchain with many of these NFTs. This promised to transform the system into a carbon-depleting form so much that it kept it working safely, but this hasn't happened yet. The timing of this switch is still unknown.

From a fairness and ethical standpoint, the choice to sell a particular art as an NFT may not have the right opportunity it has. Digital artist RJ Palmer recently warned on Twitter that there are accounts that extract art by minting tweets from fellow artists, artists, and selling them as NFTs. The work of a budding artist can be severely abused if not properly enforced or investigated whether the person writing the NFT is the real artist, the true creator, or the copyright holder. It has created an environment in which the relative anonymity of cryptocurrency transactions can be exploited, stolen and harmed.

6.3   Make enlightened business decisions

Transitioning the practice of art into cryptographic art requires careful planning as a business decision as well as the selection of art dealers and galleries. The crypto art industry is now valued at $445 million, with Nifty Gateway leading the way in terms of sales volume. Because the competition is intense, it's critical to grasp the lingo, choose the appropriate platform, and seek out well-informed professionals for guidance. Do not focus on stable or fast profit yet. It is advisable not to allocate funds from the sale of cryptographic arts to pay the rent. Thus, it won't be different from the "old" art market.

Studies show that, given the environmental impact of Ether mining, the footprint a computer needs to create a single board NFT is the same as the total electricity usage of EU residents in a month. In comparison, for the year 2020, Louvre Museum consumed same amount of electricity as 677,224 households in Paris. It would be good to invest some of the income earned from the art of cryptography to fund Jason Bailey's Green NFT grants and other attempts to decrease NFT consumption of energy.

Just as you would experiment with a new medium, experiment with one piece at a time. It's a good idea to complete, embed, or create activated encrypted art by playing it back in media, such as playing it as an animation in .mp4 or .gif format, adding sound, or converting a picture into interactive digital art. You can also create an NFTonly series to see which works are the most popular. We experiment and research what's best for your target collector and you, while staying true to your values and the brand community.

Therefore, as long as the legal consequences are understood, NFT can provide an attractive alternative to the usual art market. The choice of the market and the precise artwork to be sold is the result of precised consideration of commercial, practical and legal aspects.

7 CASES OF USE OF NON-FUNGIBLE TOKEN

Gaming

NFT is famous and well-known in the gaming world as it solves one of its inherent problem. Such as popular games like Fortnite does not allow anyone to sell rare skins, weapons, accessories and features.

With NFT, these features can be transferred and easily used in a variety of games. Thus, non-fungible tokens help promote the economy of the game.

Digital Assets

Participants in Decentraland and can purchase virtual land. ENS is another example close to home, using NFTs in the ETH domain for ease of sale and purchase.

Identity

NFTs are optimal to combat identity theft, and can represent personal information by digitizing appeerence, medical records and educational background. Digital artists can also convert their work to NFT for copyright.

Testing IDs using NFTs can convert real game tickets into non-fungible tokens and eliminate fakes.

Collectibles

NFT brings a new revolution to the world of collectibles. As a result, traditional collectors are now becoming digital assets. To understand the usage of non-fungible tokens, it is worth examining their standards and origins, which leads us back to ERC721.

Now I have listed some popular NFT use cases. The best question is that the NFT between finance, technology, sports, arts and music has not been sold. Soon all the popular names will enter the in this game. For example, Twitter co-founder Jack Dorsey sold his first tweet for $ 2.9 million on March 22. The tweet was, "I just setting up my twttr." The money was donated in charity.

A group of NFTs and art lovers bought a piece of Bansky's art, burned it down, and sold it as an NFT work for estimated US$380,000. Lindsay Lohan sold her "Lindsay `Lightning` Lohan" as her first NFT for approximately $50,000 on rarible.com (she also promised to donate the proceeds to a charity that accepts Bitcoin to empower young generation"). Rob Gronkowski sold a limited edition NFT tournament trading card for more than a million dollar. Elon Musk had a change of mind about selling a techno song about NFTs as an NFT. Steve Aoki (Dream Catcher) limited art collection sold for a total of $4.25 million, and there are still many works for sale.

Let's not forgot to mention that there is a cost of $100 for adding/listing "each" your NFT art to the Ethereum network. Unless you are famous already, you may end up with only one or two dollars as an offer for a listing that cost you $100.

7.1   What are ERC-721 tokens?

The ERC-721 token is another form of token that is created for the Ethereum network according to its smart contracts standards. At the end of 2017, a developer, Dieter Shirley, proposed the creation of this new standard, and it has been getting attention in the crypto world.

As discussed earlier, this standard was designed to create interchangeable tokens with unique and non-expendable characteristics, which will make each token unique in its entire existence and can neither be deteriorated nor destroyed.

The word ERC-721, when broken down, refers to the creation of NFTs on the Ethereum Blockchain as a means of establishing guide standards. Because of this, NTF is a sort of token that is built in accordance with the Ethereum ERC-721 specification.

NFTs can be found in a variety of decentralised networks, including Neo and EOS, in addition to the Ethereum blockchain. On the other hand, Intelligent contractability and a comprehensive set of NFT tools are required for these systems. For example, intelligent contracts enables addition of specific descriptions, like metadata, in the contract.

7.2   Important information

Art of NFT

Non-fungible tokens (NFTs) have been exploited by digital artists in order to create NFT art. However, one factor that has contributed to the increased popularity of this specialised NFT market is the amount of money that artists are able to recuperate in NFT markets

Crypto art data

The entire volume of NFT-based artwork hit $ 8.2 million during the end of 2020, according to a crypto art data and analysis platform that concentrates on Cryptocurrency's art.

This was a huge rise when compared to the previous volume of $ 2.6 million dollars every month.

The total value of the market is currently more over $ 130 billion in value. The surge in market value reflects a shift in the perception of collectors from a simple recreational activity to a significant financial movement.

According to Richard Chen, the founder of Crypto art, a rise in awareness of what non-fungible tokens may accomplish to retain authenticity has contributed to an increase in the volume of bargaining.

Artists working with digital media, in particular, were able to sell their work at some of their best prices in the last months of 2020. If the price of Bitcoin fluctuates in September 2020, a digital artwork created using NFT technology will be worth 262 ETHEREUM.

Earlier this year, another NFT designer negotiated the sale of the item for $131.250, which, at the time, was NFT's tallest product and hadn't been sold until a couple of months later. Surprisingly, the best days for NFT artists were yet to come, as a collection of NFT artworks was sold for $ 777,777.78 just two months after the auction sale.

This dramatic change in value demonstrates that the value of each token is derived from the rarity and uniqueness. Thus, non-fungible token apps such as Decentraland, CryptoKitties, CryptoPunks and many others are in great demand.

7.3 What are the Cryptokitties?

In the decentralised protocol of ETH-Powered, a popular game known as Cryptokitties allows players to gather virtual cats and sell them to other players, as well as reproduce them. As a bastion of Nft since its release at the height of that year's bull race, Blockchain of the 1990s Cult Classic Tamagotchi (in the same spirit, check out Defi'sAavegotchi!), has continued to serve as a source of inspiration for new players.

In particular, this game was the first universal use case in the largest b.lock of blocks that was devoted to leisure activities. Furthermore, the game opened the door to the possibility of DAPPs being used for recreational reasons. After its inception, Cryptokitties generated a lot of excitement across the Ethereum platform, which quickly turned into a negative thing as its popularity slowed down the network, pushing the prices up and causing transaction confirmations to take longer than expected.

Owners of Kitties and breeders of virtual cats can advertise their virtual cats through the use of clever contracts. They attract the attention of investors and serious money to non-fungible token (NFT) markets like OpenSea.

If you are a cat lover and are wondering how to purchase Cryptokitties, the process is straightforward. To begin, you'll need a Chrome or Firefox web browser, a MetaMask wallet, and some Ethereum (ETH) tokens to put in it. After that, go to the Kitties market and choose your cat. Then, pay for it and you're done.

Dapper Labs, the company that created Cryptokitties, has just followed up on its success with NBA Topshot, a market for digital memorabilia geared toward NBA fans.

7.4 What Are CryptoPunks?

In January 2021, a dark Cryptopunks "Alien" NFT WENT FAMOUS when it was sold for an incredible $ 760,000, which was the equal to 605 Ethereum at the time. Cryptopunks is famous as the first NFT series, and its breakthrough idea predates both the Cryptokitties and ERC-721 blockchains, which were both created in the same year. The outcome has been an increase in scarcity, with an average selling price of more than $ 6,000 in 2020. As explained by a spokeswoman for the investment organisation, which includes many prominent members of the DEFI sector, digital art would draw a new market of younger collectors who would appreciate it over time and eventually evolve into "iconic" digital pieces. The question "punk," number 2890, is one of the nine existing "alien" collectibles carried out by Larva Labs and was released for the last time in July 2017 for only 8 ETHE (around $ 1,500 at that time).

7.5 CoinMarketcap X the Sandbox: CMC Heroes

CoinMartcap and the Sandbox cooperated to create their own CoinMarketcap Hero NFTS line, which was released in January 2021. There are currently six CMC heroes available: CoinMarketcaptain, Protector, Hothead, Sage, Liquifier and Brawler. Because of the shortage of resources, CoinMarketcaptain can only be obtained by those who have five other heroes.

7.6 What else can be converted into an NFT?

Compliance with Yeld Farming in Defi

NFTs are beginning to intersect with decentralised finance (DEFI), specifically with agricultural techniques that create goods and services.

It was not until 2020 that the fruits of this new collaboration began to be seen in the marketplace. The Yearn Finance protocol, for example, which is a DEFI protocol, has developed an insurance product called Y. With the help of NFT approaches, Y. Insure depicts the distinctive properties of insurance contracts (ERC-721). For the most part, typical ERC-20 Tokens "didn't make sense" when used to express the specific aspects of an insurance policy.

Enjin, Bancor and Meme are examples of Defi's other ventures that have an NFT aspect.

Individual skills

Non-fungible tokens may be used to indicate the timing or ability of a person to monetize them. An NFT can be used for a variety of purposes, such as movies, podcasts and bulletins.

8   POPULAR PROJECTS

NFTs are being utilized as collectable and tradable components in a number of applications. A selection of some of the most popular will be presented.

DecentralLand.

Decentraland is a decentralised virtual reality environment in which users can trade and own virtual land as well as various other items. Cryptovoxels is a players' game for the trade, development and creation of virtual assets.

Gods Unchained

This is a collecting game in which the cards are provided on the blockchain as NFT. Players may own and trade digital cards at the same property level as physical cards since each digital card is unique.

My Crypto Heroes

It is a multiplayer role-playing game in which users may elevate historical figures by completing objectives and fighting other players. The items and heroes in the game are represented by tokens stored on the Blockchain Ethereum.

Binance Collectibles

They are non-fungible tokens (NFTs) that were created in collaboration with ENJIN and BINANCE on a specific instance. Keep an eye out for our forthcoming raffles and follow Binance on Twitter if you want to get your hands on one.

Crypto stamps

The Austrian Post Office distributed these to bridge the gap between the physical and the digital world. Like any other stamp, these stamps are used to transport letters and packages. Their automated images, on the other hand, are saved on the Ethereum Blockchain, which makes them a marketable digital collection.

8.1 Top NFT Projects

Because the NFT subspace is growing at an exponential rate, the number of NFT-related activities and objects has increased as well. They range from gaming organisations to commercial facilities affiliated with the NTF. These are five of the most significant NFT initiatives underway presently.

OpenSea: This is where most of the NFT collectibles and art are sold on a business basis. The objects that have been recorded range from ENS to virtual pets and plots of land. Surprisingly, the commercial area allows purchases to be made using a few virtual monetary forms such as DAI and ETH.

Async.Art: It is NFT's marketplace featuring programmable art. This platform's peculiarity is that the artist can create a dynamic art where the master art can be composed of different layers, and every layer can be customized.

The master is the overall work, and the layers are the layers or elements that make it up. The customers can purchase the master or single "layers."

The artist can allow specific parameters of the work to be changed by editing individual layers. The different versions of the layers are called states.

In every state, you can change color, scale, rotation, transparency, and other parameters according to the limits allowed by the artist. Only the owner of a state can modify this state, and his modification will be immediately reflected in the master.

It is also possible to set changes related to certain parameters such as time, stock market trends, and weather.

The work will therefore be "living" and will always change.

CryptoKitties: Despite the fact that we have already discussed this assignment, it deserves to be included on the list of the greatest NFT projects because it has brought the entire NFT game into the limelight.

Ethereum Name Service (ENS): This is a project for the management of area names that began in the middle of 2017. The ETH domain names are non-fungible tokens (NFTs) that follow the Ethereum ERC-721 specifications and are available on NFT commercial exchanges.

Decentraland: Decentraland is a top-tier NFT project that focuses on creating a distributed virtual world. Members can purchase virtual land in this section. Furthermore, each and every "occupant" is equipped with an advanced identification system. An NFT (non-fungible token) is a unique cryptographically produced token that makes use of blockchain innovation to connect with a unique computerised resource that cannot be replicated. An NFT is a token that is not widely used and is made infrequently.

These non-fungible tokens stand in contrast to conventional digital currencies such as Monero (XMR), Bitcoin (BTC), and Ether (ETH), which are fungible; for example, you may trade one Bitcoin for another Bitcoin. Non-fungible tokens are those that cannot be traded for other tokens.

Despite the fact that the use of NFTs has spread to a variety of various endeavours, they are most frequently associated with the gaming and advanced collectibles industries, and they are most frequently encountered as a specific Ethereum token based on the ERC-721 standard. Although their use is beginning to extend to other blockchains in 2021, such as the BEP-721 standard of the Binance Smart Chain, it will take several years before it becomes widespread.

8.2 Latest Sells of NFTs

8.2.1 NFT sold a column from 'The New York Times' for 475,000 euros.

Kevin Roose, a New York Times journalist, has sold a column in the newspaper for $ 560,000 at auction. (about 475,000 euros after turning it into an NFT (non-fungible token), a certification system of digital authenticity based on blockchain technology that has starred in some spectacular auctions recently, such as the sale of the first tweet for almost 2.5 million euros or a digital artistic composition for about 58 million euros.

The sale of Roose's column is non-profit making. In the same column that has been auctioned, which consists of describing the column's online auction project itself, it is specified that the result of the sale will be donated to Neediest Cases Fund, a charitable foundation of The New York Times itself.

After observing the phenomenon of the NFTs brought to art or the sale of NBA plays on video, Roose wondered if it could be applied to journalism, so to experiment, he consulted the newspaper and started it. The author relates that he decided to take the test after seeing how these digital certificates were spread in various fields, especially in the art world:

The column describes the process of launching the sale, which began for 24 hours and a minimum price of 0.5 Ether (a cryptocurrency like bitcoin), equivalent to about $ 850. The final result came to 350 Ether.

Even if they have paid almost half a million euros, the buyer of that first column will not have the article's copyright or any right of reproduction or retransmission. It will simply have the property title of the column in PNG image format. As a bonus, Roose promised to have the buyer's name published and to have The Daily host Michael Barbaro send him a personalized voice memo congratulating him on his purchase.

Roose's column warns that "the world of cryptocurrencies is full of scammers whose projects often fail." Additionally, critics point out that crypto-related projects and NFTs consume enormous energy and computer power, posing a threat to the environment as they grow exponentially. "The journalist considers it legitimate to wonder "what exactly NFT buyers get for their money and if those tokens will become broken links if the markets and hosting services that store the underlying files disappear."

Rose notes in her column that "it's easy to be skeptical of NFTs." *"But I'm cautiously optimistic about them,"* he concludes, "for the simple reason that they represent a new way for creative people to earn a living online."

8.3 Expensive NFTs

NFT fans see great potential in the NFT Ethereum (ETH) space. Criticism, on the other hand, believes that the NFT market is excessive and that the hype on non-fungible tokens is nothing more than hot air. Nonetheless, NFTs are already being traded for enormous sums. Let's discuss some of the most expensive non-fungible tokens available today.

8.3.1 Beeple's Digital Art Collection - $ 3.5 million

Mike Winkelmann, a CGI artist known as Beeple in the group, had the most important sales for NFT in its history. It all began with Beeple's announcement of the selling of 21 of his works on Twitter. Since his art was focused on NFTs, things moved quickly. All was also backed up by records and an accurate sample of Beeple hair.

The NFT Nifty Gateway Marketplace operated by the 'Winklevoss Brothers Gemini Exchange' received a share of sales revenue. The first 10 auctions totaled almost $900,000. Ten further works of art were purchased for a total of $1.2 million by bidders. The last painting's auction was revealed just before it began. Tim Kang auctioned it off for $ 777,777. For a total of $ 3.5 million, 21 works of art were sold. A video was shared on Twitter by the artist following the agreement, in which his pals greeted Beeple's performance with a shower of Champagne in celebration of their victory.

8.3.2 Rick and Morty ($ 2.3 million)

Justin Roiland, the creator of the renowned cartoon comedy "Rick and Morty" was among the artists who sold NFT paintings at excessive rates. His collection of 16 pieces was auctioned for ETH 1,300 (approximately $2.3 million). In his statement, Roiland explained that the auction was a means for him to push the frontiers of cryptographic art while also contributing a portion of the revenues to help poor people without homes currently living in the streets of Los Angeles.

It's worth noting that some of Roiland's artwork has been reproduced as well. The titles of works "It's Tree Guy Basically" and "Eligible Bachelor's" cost $10 and $100. Due to their rarity and originality, works of art produced in a single copy sold for a greater price—the play "The Simpsons" sold for $ 290,100. Initially, the auction's opening bid was $ 14,999, and its counterpart was sold at equal price.

8.3.3 Axie Infinity Lands- $ 1.5 million

Axie Infinity allows users to create their empire, complete with fantastic characters. Lucia is the world's name where you can purchase virtual property, and there are only a few spots available. The entire plot is split into 90,601 smaller parcels, with players owning 19% of them.

Falcon said that the land he purchased is in an excellent position. Furthermore, as shown by the rising number of active users on Axie Infinity, the trend is gradually increasing. It would also be possible to plan activities on "your territory," like concerts or festivals, in the future, and thus earn profit.

8.3.4   The Crypto Punks

A game known as "CryptoPunks" was auctioned off on the NFT for 605 ETH at the end of January. Featuring over 10,000 unique digital characters, CryptoPunks is a digital universe inspired by the crypto art movement.

They can be traded on a CyberPunks market. It should be noted that the characters in the game were originally available for free, with the only requirement being that you had an Ethereum wallet.

It is NFT # 2890, which was taken in 2017 and then sold for an astronomically high amount a few months later in 2018. It's a really rare type of 'punk' to find.

8.3.5 One F1 Delta Time track

The area of F1 Delta Time was sold for almost nine million REVV tokens. As of the time of writing this book, the REVV has climbed by 500 percent, and it would cost $ 1.2 million to produce the same amount of REVV at the current exchange rate.

It comprises 330 tokens of this kind, divided into four tiers ranging from "Rare" to "Apex." The virtual circuit for the Circuit de Monaco is constructed using these tokens. Each token comes with a virtual track share and other benefits. This specific NFT had reached the "apex" of its development. Its purchaser will earn 5% of all in-game sales and 4.2 percent of elite staking income produced by player deposits. REVV utility tokens can be used to pay for both.

8.3.6 Finance Insurance for NFT

You will get up to 5,000 ETH protection against Curve's smart contract errors thanks to a dedicated digital policy. NFT costs 350 ETH, which is currently worth over $ 560,000.

The cover is another name for Yinsure. In a nutshell, it's a combination of Nexus Mutual-guaranteed insurance and a different form of tokenized insurance. Insurance plans are defined by the letter NFT. Each one is a one-of-a-kind NFT, also known as ayNFT, that can be sold, exchanged or purchased.

8.3.7 Virtual lands in Decentraland

On the Decentralandblockchain game, someone purchased 12,600 m2 for 514 ETH. The game is a decentralized virtual reality platform based on Ethereum. Users can develop, play with, and monetize their content and applications on the platform.

LAND is a minimal 3D virtual space in Decentraland. Ethereum smart contracts manage this non-fungible digital asset, and the virtual landowner has complete power over it.

8.3.8 Land at 22.2 in Decentraland is available for purchase for 345 ETH.

Decentraland has made a resurgence in the world of technology. Another tract of land at 22.2 acres in a "great location" is up for grabs.

The size of the land in Decentraland is predetermined. Decentraland sells and leases the majority of its space, with around 80% of it being private. No one owns the remainder of the land, such as roads and squares.

Players can only walk their characters on their own land or on public land, so choosing the right location is critical. t is likely that lots in more popular areas will be more expensive than those in less popular ones.

Based on the increase of non-fungible tokens and the sold, this may be another significant trend shortly after DeFi. One of the features of NFTs is that they each have their own distinct features. While NFTs continue to be a tiny business, they provide a wide variety of applications.

8.3.9 CryptoSpaceCommanders Battlecruiser - 250 ETH

It is a space MMORPG developed by Lucid Sight. The company received a total of $ 11 million to fund the development of its "scarcity engine," a tool that would allow it to bring its Blockchain-powered games to mobile devices, Personal Computers and Consoles in the near future.

Video games are key to the mass adoption of cryptocurrencies

Ethereum is utilised to safeguard properties of game, execute all in-game contracts, and power the game's free-market economy, which operates without the need for developer.

Users can explore the world or engage in combat with other players in search of materials. Players can trade, keep or sell the retained resources to make profit at at any point in their journey.

Each ship in the game is unique and has its own set of qualities, which you may learn about through playing the game. The more valuable a ship is in terms of generating wealth in the game, the more expensive it is to purchase it in the first place.

The Battlecruiser was purchased for 250 ETH when it first appeared on the market in September of 2020.

The Battlecruiser was the world's first combat ship of its kind to be built. It has the ability to be transferred instantly anywhere on the CSC globe within 20 light-years, making it ideal for creeping up on hostile ships and launching a lethal ambush.

8.3.10 Gods Unchained (Atlas) -210 ETH

It is a competitive card game built on the Ethereum Blockchain that is similar to the hugely popular game Hearthstone in terms of gameplay and mechanics. Gods Unchained's proprietary mechanics, made possible by the game's Blockchain-based nature, are the most significant difference between the two. Players may resell the cards on the secondary market if they so choose.

Gods Unchained has been considered the world's first Blockchain-based e-sport, and it is now in its beta phase. An annual Gods Unchained World Championship will be held, with a prize pool of USD$100,000 and a 10 percent of all card pack purchases going toward the winner. The current estimated prize pool for the first Gods Unchained event is of around USD$540,865.

Since the game includes an e-sport component, players want to be as competitive as possible and develop strong decks when competing in tournaments, increasing the value of the cards.

A maximum of four "Mythic" cards with powerful abilities in the game will be released by the Gods Unchained team each year by the its team. Atlas is one of the Mythic cards, and he represents the god of the sky. It was discovered by chance in a deck of cards by a lucky player who had no idea how valuable it was. However, it wasn't until the Gods Unchained team confirmed the value of the digital treasure to the card's owner that the asset was able to capture their interest.

It took five days for the auction to conclude, with the winning bidder receiving 210 ETH. Only time will say if this is a good investment, but the early indicators are positive.

8.3.11 Gods Unchained (Prometheus) -235 ETH

As a result of great anticipation, Gods Unchained's marketplace was introduced, which resulted in a flurry of activity as players started exchanging cards.

An additional mythological card, known as the Prometheus, which had a one in a million chance of being discovered and was concealed in a random package. Given the card's one-of-a-kind characteristics, as well as its overall strength in the game, it was the ideal card for those who were serious about competing for a portion of the $ 500,000 prize pool.

Consequently, when Prometheus was placed up for sale by the player who found it, the card was in high demand, reaching a top bid of 235 Ethereum at an auction.

9 SECURITY AND NON-FUNGIBLE TOKEN

9.1 Standards for Non-Fungible Token

Because of their requirements, non-fungible tokens are extremely strong. In addition to providing developers with the assurance that assets will behave in a given manner, they also explain precisely how to interact with the assets' basic functionality.

This means that developers can create complex logic that can be applied to assets and offer them to users who may no understand how to interact with them. Standards also allow fo interoperability between multiple NFT games, which opens up the possibility of trading assets (cross-game).

There are four main standards that make NFTs work, and currently, only one organization is involved in designing standards for NFTs: the ERC-721 (Non-Fungible Token Standard). AGAME, a blockchain-based game platform created this standard in 2018. The goal of this standard is to create common rules and functionality that can be applied across every game that uses NFTs.

This allows for interoperability between all games and incentivizes developers to use this as the main NFT standard. Although some other organizations have started working on standards as well, none of them has been formally released yet. This means that ERC-721 is one of the only standards that supports NFTs and makes them work seamlessly.

Some developers make design choices based on cultural norms and values. NFTs can also be a part of these norms and values if they are allowed to look like real-world assets. For instance, certain societies in Japan have a unique way they think about non-fungible items (the same is true for many others around the world). In Japan, items as simple as chopsticks and paper are considered to be unique and valuable because of the effort that was put into creating them.

If game creators opt to utilize NFTs to include this cultural element into their games, they will be able to generate game assets that are more valuable than what players can create on their own. This is one of the ways that NFTs may outperform conventional digital products.

The real potential of NFTs lies in blockchain technology. The blockchains they run on and the tools provided by developers can either work together or be completely incompatible. There has been a significant effort in the last year to make NFTs and other blockchain technologies work together so that game creators can get more advantages and gamers can earn more value. This includes the need for numerous characters to have particular functions, such as avatars that may be transferred to other game players.

NFTs are extremely easy to create. The only requirement is to define a series of properties for it, such as name and image. These properties can then be used in the NFT's smart contract, which can handle all other details and make them work seamlessly with all other NFTs. NFTs are made on smart contracts that implement ERC-721.

NFTs are officially recognized by the Ethereum network and are therefore considered to be an Asset on the blockchain. This means that they have a unique address and ID so that they can be managed just like any other asset. The only difference is that the NFT in question will always be a unique item. This gives them a certain level of value and status – just like fiat money For example, if a user has created an NFT for their character in a game, they can be used by that player as a form of game currency.

This gives them an incentive to treat the NFT like cash and exchange it for real-world objects or services within the game (fiat). The most popular way to access non-fungible tokens is through the Ethereum blockchain. Even though there are several other projects that support NFTs, the ERC-721 standard makes NFTs work seamlessly on Ethereum. The main benefit of this is that all the tools and specifications for creating an NFT exist on the blockchain. This means that developers are highly motivated to create their own smart contracts with ERC-721 to make it easy for players to use them.

There are three main parts of the smart contract for an NFT contract: primary functionality, describing its properties, and the token interface.

The first part is the primary functionality of an NFT. This refers to what a token can do when it is created and exists within a certain game. For example, this could describe how a particular item can be used to progress in the game or what special abilities it might have.

9.1.1 Non-Fungible Tokens Metadata

As it has been discussed earlier, the smart contract has three main parts, and describing its properties is the second main part of the smart contract.

In the non-fungible token smart contract, there is a list of attributes that define the NFT properties. These include its name and ID. The next attribute is called "metadata". This is information that describes the NFT but isn't part of its properties. Attributes that can be used with this kind of metadata include "owner", "location", and "avatar".

The owner field refers to who is storing and keeping track of the NFT in question. This could be the game developer or a user. This is useful because it makes the owner of an NFT responsible for any actions that might be taken in relation to it, such as transferring it to another player or destroying it, for example. The next field is the location, and since there may be some game mechanics that depend on having this information available, location could have many different meanings and interpretations depending on what kind of game is being developed. For example, "location" could simply indicate the position of an item in a scene. It might also refer to the position of an item relative to other items in a game.

An item might have a special "location" that determines when it is safe to interact with it. It could also be used to indicate the current condition of an item.

The metadata field is used to describe any special details about an NFT that are not stored in the properties or defined through other attributes, such as its name and image. These details can include aspects such as creation time, creator, and image ID.

The final part of the NFT smart contract is called the token interface. This refers to how different smart contracts can interact with an NFT. It is useful for game developers because it makes it possible for them to create new NFTs without having to make any changes to their initial code. Using the token interface, they can create a new "monster" (for example) and give it a certain combat power. They can then include these details in the NFT's metadata. This means that new items can be created without having to create specific points or levels. This creates more possibilities in terms of game mechanics and design, which makes smart contracts more powerful and useful.

9.2 Be smart about copyright

Any artist should know how and when to utilize copyright because it is a bedrock of intellectual property, especially when it comes to NFTs.

In the USA it is not necessary to register with the copyright office to exist, however, to apply against others it is necessary. The Copyright Act of 1976 provides for the exclusive replication, distribution and production of works by authors of pictures, sculptures or graphics. Platforms have to establish methods to deal with violating materials. However, it is easy to record a visual arts work within a couple of minutes, ideally before it is published.

While it is tempting to convert pre-existing images into an NFT, doing so without significant alteration and a clear additional message is like walking on a tightrope. Converting a digital artwork without the author's express permission may result in litigation, with the offender arguing that the use is "fair" under copyright law. Courts will evaluate the resemblance between the original and defendant's works, the market in which the parties operate, and the purpose and transformative character of the defendant's work when making fair-use judgments. A licencing agreement can avert complications and provides a fantastic opportunity to communicate with other creators.

Furthermore, artists should be informed that unless a written agreement between the customer and the artist is signed, the NFT purchaser does not have the right to replicate the underlying work purchased from them. However, any NFT platform may grant itself a non-exclusive, global, and royalty-free licence to distribute and reproduce copies of the art offered for sale by using the Terms & Conditions of the platform. The unfortunate reality is that these terms are rarely if ever negotiable.

9.3 Keeping your information safe

For artists, linking an NFT to a platform that accepts Ether is essential. Digital currencies can be stored in software wallets (like MetaMask or Coinbase) or hardware wallets (like hard drive). Because of increased protection against hacking (internet fraud), hardware wallets are a better long-term investment that has been shown to be more reliable.

When selecting a cryptocurrency wallet, it is recommended to look for two-factor verification, a secure way to store your seed phrase (same as password), and the ability to send and receive payments (same as debit card number). It is also advisable to get into the habit of using a virtual private network (VPN) while trading cryptocurrencies. It is also recommended that artists examine which wallets are accepted by the NFT platform before creating their own (for example, Foundation uses MetaMask).

10 NFT FOR PHOTOGRAPHY

10.1 Photography And Digital World

Chemically developed light-sensitive emulsions have been the age of photography in the early 1900s, limiting the skills and usage of photography. The recent technology in photography can only be imagined by a maniac then. The 21st century digital age has brought a lot to the photography world. The shift to digital storage and capture technology from the early 1900s was started in the late 80's when the first consumer digital cameras were introduced and Photoshop was first released in 1990. The program (Photoshop) extended the conventional darkroom by extensively using the classic instruments of two-color pictorial photography (black and white) and also allowed photographers to go deeper into their creative explorations. The long-standing beliefs about photographic documentary or veracity "truth value" were nearly dispelled when technology enabled photographers to readily alter the structure and even the substance of an image. To some people, the very nature of the medium has been changed, but the best is yet to happen.

The first decade of this century was when photographers and the world felt the full impact of digital photography – its usage, how it creates fantastic memories, and some business usage like marketing. It was still common practise in 2001 to use old film cameras to shoot breaking news events. The fast transmission and simple digital pictures led to the shift of journals and magazines into a digital method of operating and put digital cameras in the hands of its photographers geared to pros. The widespread use of digital photography has prompted a variety of responses from photographers such as Jerry Spagnoli, Deborah Luster, Chuck Close Sally, and Mann. Some have reverted to traditional photographic processes such as daguerreotyping or working with wet-collodion plates, which is a photographic process that dates back to the nineteenth century.

Some other photographers, such as Alison Rossiter and Chris McCaw, have resorted to using antiquated enlarging paper from the mid-20th century for their work and printing it themselves. This was on the verge of reviving popularity in the art world, but it was projected to be rendered obsolete by the availability of widely available web photographs.

Others used this time to think critically on the new picture environment they were in. Pictures of light trails made by some satellites, such as Trevor Paglen, were taken as you traveled across the night sky. The convergence of pictures and videos still-digital and web design tools allowing audio editing, animation, and movement control also led to an arena in which photography was an instrument and a tool for the creation of multimedia experiences. In the 21st century, photography became online digital communication into the contemporary art world, transcending its previously distinct character and significantly boosting its importance as a means of visual communication.

With widely accessible internet pictures, photo books can now be simply produced. Digital printing, moreover, reduced the publishing costs while enabling photographers to choose how their ideas were presented, both in story and context. The digital presence of photography can not be neglected, and its usage in the digital world is fascinating, but people needed more. People need to feel that their digital image is not just out there on the Internet; they want value for their work. Hence, the creation of NFTs.

You must be wondering what an NFTs was; don't be surprised because it is just an acronym.

10.2 Meaning Of NFT For Photographer

Non-Fungible Tokens (also known as digital tokens or certificates) are digital tokens or certificates that are saved on a secure distributed database and cannot be forged (blockchain). As a result, NFTs are one-of-a-kind digital assets that can be purchased and sold on a trustless platform, with each transaction being permanently stored on the blockchain.

Another way to think of NFT is as a certificate of authenticity that is permanently included into a database, which includes any future transactions in which ownership is swapped or transferred. You will be able to see for the rest of time who founded the NFT, who purchased it, and so on. NFT is a unique technology that holds a great deal of promise but has yet to be fully explored.

The NFT can be thought of as a certificate of authenticity that is permanently stored in a database, which is then used to record any subsequent transactions in which ownership is exchanged or transferred. From now on, you can see who started the NFT, who bought it, and so forth. NFT is a one-of-a-kind technology that offers a tremendous deal of potential, but which has not yet been completely investigated. When we talk about blockchain, we are referring to the underlying technology that powers decentralised cryptocurrencies such as Ethereum and Bitcoin. Currently, NFTs are not completely supported on all blockchain technologies due to the fact that blockchain technology is still in its early stages and that each blockchain has a unique structure. Ethereum appears to be the most extensively utilised blockchain service for NFTs at the moment, but this is susceptible to change as the technology matures. Even though

10.4 Digital Art And Physical Art Worlds – The Difference

Starting with the physical world and how selling printed copies of your photography works in artwork with the usage of excellent cameras.

Obviously, you have to select one or a collection of your photographs to print as a physical copy. After the selection process is printing, and at this stage, you have to decide their edition. In simple words, you have to determine their availability in the market; hence, the value will be appreciated. You are deciding if you are printing only one version – edition of one – or an edition of 10, 50, or more. You can also decide to have an open edition, which means you have no limit concerning the number of times you can print and distribute your photograph.

The next thing is to give every print a signature, which is more like an edition number and an authenticity certificate. This certificate is your proof of ownership and your authorization for its distribution. Simply put, it shows that the print is real. This will also allow collectors to prove their ownership of the editioned print.

Imagine a scenario that someone walks into your gallery and snaps a high-resolution image of your collections, then the person decided to print it out and started posting it to be real. Your proof of ownership can only be established with your certificate. This is exactly what NFTs do as well.

Now let's apply our scenario to the digital world. Take NFTs as your signature or your authenticity certificate – deed of ownership. In the case of the digital world, you can also decide how much scarcity you want, and blockchain technology will make sure that the counterfeit can never be produced.

So, when you "mint" and "convert your art into NFT," you are establishing your right of possession of the art and how many editions of the image you want to be available. Then, the blockchain technology will control and keeps a record of how the digital art exchange hands – who buys and owns your art.

10.5 Photographers And Other Digital Artists – How Can They Benefit From NFT Technology?

The conventional market for photography and other digital art has been limited to printmaking, stock photography licensing, and other avenues of selling physical copies or non-physical rights to a work of art. With huge market congestion in the last decade, it is increasingly difficult for most artists to make money from their work, but NFTs is presenting an entirely new market and mindset for artists and photographers. Interested buyers in art and technology are now looking to support their favorite artists and acquire scarce digital assets that can increase in value. NFTs are like aid to photographers/artists and buyers alike due to the unique structure of the trustless blockchain technology. Each transaction is recorded for everyone to see and cannot be erased, misplaced, or undone. Artists can also benefit from the secondary market by including a particular percentage or commission in their NFTs that will be paid to them on any subsequent sales of their NFT. Most importantly, artists can hold on to their full copyright, unlike many licensing agreements.

10.6 How Can Photographers Use/Create NFTs?

Converting or tokenizing digital art (it can be an image or anything) is a simple process that entails uploading and placing it for sale. NFTs marketplaces are managed within the blockchain, which requires cryptocurrencies like Ethereum or Bitcoin.

For photographers, after your image has been uploaded as an NFT, several verification steps will be required, like if you are selling multiple editions or original. You can even place a royalty – a commission for the photographer upon subsequent sales – on your NFTs, like 10-15% of all future sales, just as discussed earlier.

As said by Dinch, "With respect to photography, you have the ability to convert a photograph as a token, and this photograph is own by whoever owns this token. People can download or look at it, but there is only one owner."

A landscape photographer based in Michigan, Bryan Minear, has always kept a close eye on the crypto space. He did an NFT drop that is featuring five photographs ranging from 200 to 2,500 dollars. Within few minutes, he almost sold out everything.

He commented that he was crying by the end of the day. And furtherly said that it's not like transformational money, but when you create for the love of photographs, and then that moment of validation finally arrived, which is, someone, somewhere loves your work so much that they're willing to spend some money to acquire it, it's another level of satisfaction

Minear furtherly gave the reason he chose to hold on to NFTs; he said that he realized crypto was here to stay despite different speculation that the NFT market is a bubble.

However, he doesn't see NFTs as a medium to eradicate the potential of copyright, neither does he sees the blockchain as a way to control the distribution of his work online; rather, he sees a new opportunity to reach a passionate audience about digital art and willing put value on it.

10.7 How Do Photographers Determine The Cost Of Their NFT?

This was one of the biggest obstacles for most photographers before listing their NFTs on the marketplace. Artists decide the value of their NFT as they wish. According to Minear, he said that he initially had to list his photos at a lower price to make them accessible, but he realized he didn't have enough data to make a more informed judgment because his art quickly sold out.

Then comes the big question, what is the difference between selling limited edition physical prints and selling multiple versions of an NFT?

The biggest difference between selling multiple versions of the photograph as an NFT and selling a limited edition hard copy of a photograph is tangibility.

For Minear, it also comes down to his audience values. Do they want digital ownership or a physical poster on a wall? He then noted how he sold more value as a digital print than physical prints.

10.8 Copyright And Licensing

As previously stated, copyright in photography is the same as it is in other fields; the original work's owner will always be the original work's owner, regardless of whether an NFT of that work has been sold. NFTs are digital reproductions of original works – not physical prints – and the original author retains complete control over the licensing of their work.

10.9 Can NFT Offer More Than Photography?

Photography is quite similar to Video making. Videos are images in fast motion or a series of images played in a particular order or sequence at a specified time frame or rate, usually from software playing video (digital) or device (analog).

Can NFT actually offer more to Video making than photography? This is a bigger question that needs to be unravelled.

11 NFT FOR VIDEO MAKER

Joseph Niepce was the first person to take a black-and-white picture in 1826. Joseph Plateau, a few years after (1832), became the first to simulate motion images in his invention named phenakistoscope ("spindle viewer").

In reaction to new technology, video production has continuously evolved from the earliest days of "motional pictures" more than a century ago. As long as new tools, formats and platforms are now widely recognized, every creative who works with video has to adapt.

While the way we see videos has changed continuously with technological innovation, distribution techniques and the creation of videos also need to continue in order to stay pace with this quickly changing environment. Over time, new video technology, job roles and the fundamental manner in which businesses integrate video into their broader strategy for commercial success have affected production processes. The digital video did not stop the change of television broadcasting, the video did not kill the radio star, and TV did not cease the creation of films.

On the contrary, the more than one century of film and video creation that before it laid the way for today's video environment is feasible. It has always been essential to adjust to new technologies, whether the future of video, to watch a video with a growing number of technology and media and many new tools and platforms to produce and distribute it.

11.1 How Can A Video Creator Use/Create NFTs?

The world feels like it's rapidly changing during the pandemic period, and Non Fungible tokens have come on the radar recently with Digital Artists such as Beeple making as much as $69 million for an image file. Now seems to be the best period to actually learn some essential information about creating an NFT as a Video Maker. As a Video Maker, there are potentially many benefits if you can mint and offer your artwork for sale. Cryptocurrency technology will certify you as the original owner on the blockchain and continue to pay you some royalties (Just as discussed in the case of photography).

Basically, anything in the support file formats under a 100MB JPG, SVG, PNG, GLTF, GIF, MP4, WAV, WEBM, GLB, MP3, OGG can be created. As a Video Maker, you are likely to create a good video that's below 100MB. You have the option to give unlockable content when someone purchases the NFT through an external link to another platform. Creating your video content can be done using any video-creating software. The final step is to mint the video by a platform available and put it up for sale.

11.2 What Can You Sell?

You can definitely sell anything digital from tweets, contracts, images, video skit, an album, any audio, 3d model e.t.c. Some platforms accept the following file formats: JPG, SVG, PNG, GLTF, GIF, MP4, WAV, WEBM, GLB, MP3, OGG. With a maximum file size of 100 MB

11.3 Platforms To Sell Your NFT

Presently, there are many platforms on the Internet, and they all have their advantages and disadvantages, depending on what you are selling. Some of the platforms are: SuperRare, Foundation, VIV3, OpenSea, Axie Marketplace, Rarible, BakerySwap, Nifty Gateway, and NFT ShowRoom

OpenSea seems to be better in terms of file size because they accept files up to 100MB, unlike Rarible where the maximum file size that can be uploaded is 30MB. Another advantage is that they seem to be one of the larger NFT marketplaces that don't require an invite, unlike other platforms like Niftygateway and Superrare that require invites. They also offer some fantastic free information on using their platform.

11.4 Related NFT Video Sales

NFT has been very popular recently that everyone wants to mint their artwork (Image, Music, or Video) on supported platforms to get some returns. NFT created from an image seems to be the most popular, and other digital arts are just getting some attention from creators.

One of the most popular NFT video clips is a 10-second video clip that sold for a whopping $6.6 million at the NFT auction. Pablo Rodriguez-Fraile, a Miami-based art collector, spent over USD$67,000 on a 10-second video in October 2020. The video could have been watched online without cost because we live in a technologically sophisticated age where everything is now available on the Internet, but he chose to spend USD$67,000 to obtain the video for his personal collection rather than do so. In February 2021, he sold the property for a total of 6.6 million dollars.

As discussed in NFT by photographer, the blockchain was used to authenticate the video created by a digital artist known as Beeple, whose real name is Mike Winkelmann, "the blockchain is a trustless platform that serves as a digital signature to verify and certify who owns it and that it is the original work".

Another popular NFT video that got people's attention is the LeBron James slam dunk that was sold for $208,000.

The launch of the U.S. NBA's Top Shot website has been said to be the start of the rush for NFTs, it is possible to trade, sell or buy NFTs in the form of video highlights from games on the website, which is open to anybody who is interested.

The platform says it has hit over 10,000 users buying NFT with nearly $250 million of sales. The NBA is also said to have been receiving royalties on every sale on the marketplace. And February 2021 is said to be the highest sales on the platform so far, with a total sales of over $198 million, which multiplies January's sales of $44 million.

The biggest transaction on February 22 on the platform is when a user paid $208,000 for LeBron James slam dunk video.

During an interview with one big NFT investor, known as "Pranksy," he stated that he had put USD$600 in an early NFT project in 2017, and that his portfolio of NFTs and cryptocurrencies is now worth a total of seven figures to him. Pranksy claims to have spent more than a million dollars on Top Shot and made approximately 4.7 million dollars from the resale of his various collections of the game.

You must be wondering this is it; NFT has nothing to offer another industry except an industry that involves graphics like image or video, but NFT has not stopped there; it is available for anything digital technology, even music. How can music be displayed as an NFT? Well, it is like owning an album of music as one of your collections.

12 NFT FOR MUSICIANS AND DJ

The music industry got its start approximately a century ago, when technological advances made it possible to record, store, and playback sound. Since its inception, the business has responded to several technological improvements in sound technologies, which have progressed from mono to high-fidelity stereo. Meanwhile, storage media technologies in the music industry progressed from vinyl to cassettes, and then onto compact discs and mini-discs. Then there was the evolution of gadgets that were used to replay sound, which culminated in what we have today: portable audio players. While these transformations are taking place, industry players have either had to quickly adjust to the new changes brought about by modern technologies in the industry or have simply disappeared. The music industry in the twenty-first century is currently undergoing significant transformations, which are being fueled by the rapid expansion of the integration of audio and computing technologies, as well as the Internet.

After the integration of computing technology and audio technologies, the industry was transformed into one that produces information products. The way music and songs are purchased and used in today's culture has been transformed by technological advancements. In addition, they gave ways to compose music at a low cost that can be easily made at home, mix and dub music, as well as the use of balancing and digital noise filters to improve the sound's quality. All of these things were did noy exist just a few years ago.

Digital technologies such as mp3 have established itself as a standard format. Many music software developers are satisfied with the MP3 format. Now, these files can be to a very small size, which makes it easier to send music over the Internet. With the advent of compression technology, music files may now be compressed to a very small size, making it easier to distribute music over the Internet. The introduction of the mp3 format resulted in the development of portable audio devices that allows downloading music directly from hard disks and the Internet. Music listeners can easily distribute and download music over the Internet because mp3 does not have an anti-piracy feature (pirated and legal copy).

We were told that the Internet was going to save the music industry by allowing musicians to have control on their songs and make an honest career without being tied to any industrial music complex. This hasn't benefited the artist at all.

Musicians get an estimated of 12% of profits from sales or streams. The rest goes to intermediaries.

The Covid-19 pandemic forced all musicians to abandon their tour plans in early 2020. Several artists were not earning anything because of the pandemic. In the end, they began to ask why they were working in a business where a major portion of all streaming income went to a few top musicians, and the rest went to someone else.

All of these disappointments prompted a rapid adoption of the new technology that has been circulating in the digital world; it may seem to outside observers that the music business has grown obsessed with "NFT," but it is really necessary to preserve their sweat and labor.

Many transactions have happened in the NFT-Music transaction, and millions of dollars have been made as a profit. Grimes, an EDM concept artist, sold USD$5.8 million in NFTs in February. 3LAU, another hot EDM/DJ remixer just sold USD$11.6 million in NFTs. Even more impressive: Kings of Leon released an entire album as an NFT. The DJ/Dance sensation, Steve Aoki also made USD$4.25 million in NFTs.

Here is a concise list of artists that have been making NFT and Music industry worth talking about and making an insane splash in the music world:

3Lau	$11 Million
Grimes	$6 Million
Kings of Leon	$2 Million
Steve Aoki	$4.2 Million
Odeza	$2.1 Million

VÉRITÉ	$12,000
Lil Miquela	$82,000
Pussy Riot	$200,000
Young and Sick	$865,000
Zack Fox	$15,000
Ozuna	$11,000+
Intro to Music Theory	$12,000+

You must now be wondering what they are actually selling for them to have been making this huge amount of money. They have been selling mostly short music videos, fan experiences (either during the artistic process itself or looks backstage), and digital "collectible" versions of a record, and all of which the collectors could display, sell or withhold to show the value of the artist to them.

Example of what has been sold are:

Kings of Leon - front-row tickets for life

RAC - NFT to a cassette tape tied to the NFT

3Lau- Physical waveform sculpture tied to the NFT

Intro to Music Theory - NFT-linked t-shirts scannable to their music streaming

Snoop Dogg - Digital Joint Art

Various - Unreleased tracks, exclusive music videos, digital art inspired by their music.

12.1 General Pricing Guide For Digital Artists

After reading every part of the book up to to this section, I believe you must be asking how can I start? When will I be able to sell my NFT at a high cost? Do I need to start competing with top established artists in terms of price or better under-price my NFT? The solution to these questions is highlighted below.

1. When starting as a new artist in the NFT industry, it is best to start with humility, then steadily raise your floor and consistently. The daily exchange in blockchain technology is enough to mislead any newbie, but as you continue to sell more frequently and steadily, you can raise your price. Sales are like your review; it shows your artwork is worth having as a collection.

2. Don't be too hastily to hit the 7 – 9 figures. Slow and steady is essential because the value of your artistry, especially long-term, isn't about a sale in the immediate, but how strong you have built your network. When you observe that your work isn't hitting many sales, it doesn't mean you have to burn your

tokens; just hold tight, trust the process, keep the vision clear, and keep working.

3. As mentioned earlier, the marketplace is big, and there are many platforms where you can sell your artwork, make use of all of these platforms, but be consistent with your pricing. Don't forget that you can sell your artwork on any platform regardless of where it is minted. Collectors are spread across all of these platforms, so it is best to reach as many collectors as possible.

4. Don't be afraid to play with the pricing. Sometimes you need that bold side to come out big; if it receives huge sales, it is a win-win case. Don't be afraid of making mistakes; we only learn through mistakes.

5. ETH is not a fiat system of exchange. The value of one ETH is multiple to any currency in the fiat system. So, beware of undervaluing yourself because you're thinking in terms of fiat currency – government-issued currency.

12.2 What Are Charged Particles?

Before discussing anything further, let's see what charged Particles are. It allows users to give ERC-20 tokens into an NFT.

A scarce NFT (e.g. Collectible, Art, In-Game Item, Virtual Real Estate, etc.) can be transformed into a holding for other tokens.

It is now possible to deposit any ERC-20 token into ANY NFT, but it is noted in their forum, "for yield — Aave's aTokens will be the fundamental interest-bearing asset available in the Charged Particles Protocol when we go live."

Benefit for NFTs.

Yield-bearing aTokens with programmable charge is among many assets that NFTs can hold. If you have a number of LP Tokens, speculative tokens or social tokens, you can deposit any/all of them inside a scarce NFT, and it is all possible.

In addition, it will be easy to deposit tokens/assets into other user's NFTs. It is more like having your NFT wallet.

Customization of the NFTs configurations of their NFTs is now very easy — Required Mechanics for Charged Particles include:

Time-Locks: NFT assets can only be withdrawn after a specified duration.

Charge: Aave aToken supported asset will be swapped instantly, and you can then decide how you would like to treat the interest. E.g., a particular charge can be discharged to any different address depending on your choice — the NFT creator, a charity, or a friend.

Discharge: This is when you want to remove accrued interest – configurations.

Mass (Principle) Removal Configurations: Do you have to burn the NFT to remove the principle from the NFT?

However, by using charged Particles to construct NFTs, you are enabling them to have a programmable interest and readily hold other ERC-20 tokens.

12.3 Related Concerns To Nft Technology

It is worth noting that all new technology presents concerns while growing, and one of the concerns to NFTs is that anyone can mint them. For digital artists and photographers, this is problematic because there is no legal precedent to guide sellers and buyers currently. For example, if someone downloads an image that is not theirs – they do not own the copyright, they can still mint an NFT with that image. The copyright owner would rightfully have an issue with another person profiting off their work without proper permission, but the recourse they would have is still unclear at this time. With the large volume of sales on marketplaces every day, this could pose a serious issue for the marketplaces and artists. Who gets to pay in the event of copyright infringement? Who is liable? What constitutes copyright infringement? These are all legal questions that are yet to be answered.

Another threat to NFTs is the inherent carbon footprint of blockchain and crypto technology, which is damaging the atmosphere. For the eco-conscience, this is a serious concern because the blockchain and its related technologies require enormous computing power, which means huge power consumption.

To cap it all, each marketplace has been said to have its own vulnerabilities. There have been reports of NFT vanishing from marketplaces without any notice, and this could be a significant problem if it occurs after paying minting fees or buying NFTs. The market is still gaining audience day by day, which means there may be some potential concerns out there that is waiting around the corner to be noticed.

13 PLATFORM TO SELL NFT AND ITS REQUIREMENT

After discussing the popular projects that use NFTs and the relationship between NFTs and other art (Photography, Video Maker, and Musicians and Dj), it is pertinent to discuss the platforms that support the trading of NFTs. Some of these platforms have been discussed in the previous chapter, but their requirements and how to trade NTFs on these platforms will be discussed further in this chapter.

Here is a list of platforms that allows easy trading of your Non-Fungible Tokens (NTFs).

1. OpenSea: www.opensea.io

2. Rarible: www.rarible.com

3. SuperRare: www.superrare.co

4. Foundation: www.foundation.app

5. Atomic Market: www.wax.atomicmarket.io

6. Myth Market: www.myth.market

7. BakerySwap: www.bakeryswap.org

8. KnownOrigin: www.knownorigin.io

9. Enjin Marketplace: www.enjin.io/software/marketplace

10. Portion: www.portion.io

11. Async Art: www.async.art/

13.1 OpenSea

OpenSea boasts of being the world's biggest NFT marketplace. Collectibles, sports, virtual worlds, trading cards, domain names that are censorship-resistant and art are among the non-fungible tokens available. ERC721 and ERC1155 properties are included. Unique digital assets such as Axies, ENS titles, CryptoKitties, Decentraland, and more are available to purchase, sell, and discover. They have over 700 projects, ranging from collectible games and trading card games to name systems and interactive art projects like ENS (Ethereum Name Service).

Using OpenSea's item minting tool, creators can build their objects on the blockchain. It helps you to create a set and NFTs without writing a single line of code. For example, you can link to OpenSea by creating a smart contract for an online game, or a digital item on the blockchain.

You can sell something on OpenSea for a set price, a falling auction listing or a price listing.

13.2 Rarible

It is an NFT (non-fungible token) marketplace owned by community using ERC-20 RARI token as an ownership token. Variable rewards active users who purchase or sell on the NFT marketplace with the RARI token. Per week, it distributes 75,000 RARI.

The website prioritises art assets. Rarible allows developers to "mine" fresh NFTs to sell movies, art, CDs, music and books. Those that visit Rarible can see a preview of the product, but only the customer is permitted for accessing entire project.

You can buy and sell NFTs in several categories like domains, music, sports, metaverses, memes, photography, art, and many others.

13.3 SuperRare

SuperRare is primarily a marketplace for limited-edition and unique digital artworks. Tokenized works of art created by network artists that you can own and trade. They describe themselves as a hybrid of Christie and Instagram's, offering a new way to engage with collecting, culture and art on the web.

Every art available on SuperRare is a digital collectible, a digital item that is encrypted and tracked on the blockchain. On top of the marketplace, SuperRare has created a social network. Digital collectibles are suitable for a social atmosphere because they have a clear record of ownership.

The Ethereum network's native Cryptocurrency, ether, is used in all transactions.

A form can be used to submit your artist profile and be evaluated for SuperRare's future full launch.

13.4 Foundation

It is a niche forum that brings together digital developers, crypto natives, and enthusiasts to advance the culture. It is dubbed the "new creative economy." It is mainly concerned with digital art.

In their initial blog post on their website in August 2020, they invited developers to experiment with value and Crypto and value. "Hack, subvert, and abuse the value of art," they advised.

In other words, when a collector resells their work to an other person for a better price, the artist receives 10% of the sales value.

13.5 AtomicMarket

It is an NFT market smart contract with mutual liquidity that is used by several websites. Anything available on one place appears on every other place, which is known as shared liquidity.

It's a platform for Atomic Assets, a non-fungible token standard based on the EOSIO blockchain. A standard for tokenizing and building digital assets that may be used on the Atomic Assets marketplace can be employed.

You can both search and list for NFTs for sale on AtomicMarket. Genuine and well-known NFTs collections are recognised with a verification checkmark. Malicious collections are blacklisted.

13.6 Myth Market

It is a collection of user-friendly online marketplaces for a variety of digital trading card firms. Shatner, KOGS.Market Pepe.Market and Heroes.Market are all places where you can buy digital Garbage Pail Kids cards.

This is the featured markets at the moment (for memorabilia relating to William Shatner.)

13.7 BakerySwap

BakerySwap is a decentralised exchange (DEX) and Binance Smart Chain automated market maker (AMM) that operates on the Binance Smart Chain (BSC). It uses the platform's native BakerySwap token (BAKE). It is a multi-functional crypto centre including a a range of DeFi services, an NFT supermarket and crypto launchpad.

With BAKE tokens, it offers NFT, meme contests and digital art. When you combine NFTs, you gain BAKE tokens Moreover, it is simple to mint and sell.

13.8 KnownOrigin

KnownOrigin is an online marketplace for exclusive digital artwork. Each digital art on KnownOrigin is unique. Creators can use the forum to display their piece of art and sell it to collectors. Protected by Ethereumblockchain.

Users can upload jpeg or GIF files to the KnownOrigin gallery, which is kept on IPFS.

13.9 Enjin Marketplace

An exploration and trade platform for blockchain properties. A NFT marketplace powered by Enjin. Until now, Enjin Coin has been used to purchase 2.1 billion NFTs valued USD$43.8 million. 832.7K deals have been made. The Enjin Wallet makes it easy to sell and buy gaming items.

For example, the Age of Rust and The Six Dragons multiverse and have gamified reward systems including NFT's (such as Binance and Swissborg) Microsoft Azure Heroes and community-created items.

13.10 Portion

It is an online Blockchain-based trading place that enables collectors and artists to own, sell and invest in collectibles and art quickly and transparently. This initiative is supported by Artist Collective, a decentralised global network of content creators and artists.

Portion makes it easy to collect. Cryptocurrency can be exchanged for collectibles and art at one spot.

These ERC-20 tokens are used to vote and rule on the blockchain's future. Potential and existing team members receive new tokens. Artists who generate new NFTs receive new Portion Tokens worth 500 PRT.

13.11 Async Art

Async Art is a blockchain-based creative movement. Programmable art can be created, collected, and exchanged. Both "Masters" and "Layers" are available for purchase. Layers are the different components that create the Master image. The artist decides what special abilities each layer should have. Whoever owns the Master picture will see any changes made to a Layer. Artists determine the parameters of their work and offer collectors complete control over every element. Users might, for example, change the context, a character's location, or the sky's colour.

14 HOW TO CREATE NFTS

You must be wondering that NFTs are very good investments and would like to own some. The previous chapters gave us insight into how NFTs works and some popular projects that they are used for. It's time to create a Non-Fungible Token. But before we create NFTs, let's discuss some problems that are associated with them.

14.1 Problems with the NFT

Non-fungible tokens are not without flaws, despite their impact on various businesses. Unfortunately, your issues stem from the its source - blockchain.

Decentralized networks aren't perfect, but developers are attempting to fix them. For example, verifying validity, selling buying, and storing an NFT all require some knowledge o Blockchain technology.

The problem arises because most people are only intereste in the product and not the technology behind it.

When it comes to NFTS adoption, Beeple, an NFT creator who sold some of his works for USD$66,666 cooler (and a record-breaking purchase of more than USD$777,777,777), observes that "the required infrastructure is in place," which would provide a great experience for customers.

The same goes for "Internet" and "smartphones." Most individuals have idea how these two work, but billions use them everyday. As with blockchain, we need the same experience in this case too.

Generating your own NFT artwork, as a photograph or a GIF, is a simple process that doesn't require much crypto knowledge. NFT can be used to create collectibles and other digital card sets.

You must first decide which blockchain you wish to utilize to create your NFTs. The most widely used blockchain platform for publishing NFTs is Ethereum.

However, other blockchains are gaining popularity, such as:

- Binance Smart Chain
- WAX.
- Flow by Dapper Labs
- Cosmos

- Polkadot

- Tezos

- EOS

- Tron

Each blockchain is compatible with its own standard NFT token as well as its wallet services and its markets. You can only sell NFTs on sites that take up Binance Smart Chain characteristics if you are using a Binance Smart Chain. That implies that you cannot sell it on an Ethereumblockchain-based platform like the VIV3 developed on the Flow blockchain o OpenSea.

Use one of various NFT-centric platforms to link your walle and upload the file or image you want to convert.

Ethereum NFT marketplaces are:

- Rarible

- Mintable

- OpenSea

Making NFTs on Makersplace is also possible, but you mu first register as an artist.

Mintable, Rarible, and OpenSea all have a 'Create' button.

This is how it works on OpenSea, the world's biggest NFT market in Ethereum.

To add your Ethereum wallet, click the blue "Create" button.

With your wallet password, the app connects your wallet to the marketplace. A digitally signed message in your Ethereum wallet will be required to transmit funds, but you can simply click to confirm your wallet address. The marketplace will immediately associate your wallet with your wallet password as soon as you input it when asked. To make sure your Ethereum wallet address is correct, simply click to check. There is no fee for the digital signature of a message. To prove that you are managing the wallet, this is just a demonstration.

The next move on OpenSea is to pick "My Collection" by hovering over "Create" in the top right corner. Then, as shown below, press the blue "Create" button.

When you arrive at the window, you will be guided to it, where you may name your artwork, provide a description, and submit it.

To complete this step, you will just need to create a folder for your freshly produced NFTs.

It will appear as shown below once you've assigned a picture to your set (blue). Click the pencil icon in the top right corner to add a banner image (red).

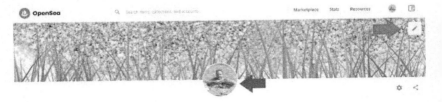

The finished result should have the same appearance as the sample to the right.

You will now be the first to create a new kind of NFT. Clicking the "Connect New Thing" button will cause your wallet to be used to sign a new message (blue).

Your NFT artwork will display in a new window.

The rarity and originality of your NFT on OpenSea and other markets should be increased. Creators may also have unlockable content that the purchaser can only access. Passwords to such utilities, coupon codes, and contact details are all examples of this.

On the Ethereum-based OpenSea platform, NFT traits are available.

When you're done, go to the bottom of the page and click "create" to confirm the NFT's presence by signing another message in your wallet.

14.2 Creation cost of an NFT

Some platforms demand a fee for creating NFTs on OpenSea. In Ethereum-based systems, this charge is called "gas.". Ether gas is the quantity of ether required to complete a certain blockchain function. That will be the launch of a new NFT to the market. Gas prices vary according to network congestion. The cost of gas prices rises as more people transfer value over the network,

Here's a helpful hint: Over the weekend, when transaction volume decreases, the cost of using Ethereum decreases somewhat. This can help you save money if you're selling multiple NFTs.

14.3 How to create and sell NFT of digital art

The configuration process varies per NFT type. If you want to configure Digital NFTs Art, you can use Opensea, a popular online seizure.

Create a digital wallet to hold Crypto and NFT. OpenSea suggests a meta mask wallet addon for Chrome.

Next, go to OpenSEA and click on my profile in the upper right corner.

Enter then follow the screen prompts to finish configuring your account.

After that, go to your account at the top right and click my collections.

Then create a new collection, click create, and enter the details.

Now, click Add new item, and you will be prompted to name your NFT and update the information.

Finally, click Create to finish.

Before listing anything on OpenSEA, sellers must first pay a gas price, which is the Ethereum Blockchain transaction cost.

OpenSea is one of the most popular NTF markets today, although Rarable and SuperRare are also fantastic choices. Artists can use them to make money on the crypto market while also reaching new audiences.

14.4 How are NFTs used?

NFTs can be used to show the value and scarcity of digital assets or other commodities. They can represent and receive everything from virtual games to artwork.

Non-fungible tokens are bought and sold in a digital market, not on regular exchanges.

14.5 What can NFTs do?

NFTS can be used with DAPPs to create Crypto collections and unique digital products. Investment product or a billable item.

The economic game is not new. Besides that, considering that many online games are already economical, blockchain adoption to tokenize game assets adds marvel. In reality, NFTs can reduce or eliminate the general inflation issue of many games. The tokenization of real-world assets is another fascinating use of NFT. As a blockchain token, this NFT can represent a real-world asset fraction. This can help many markets that lack liquidity, such as rare collection items, real estate, art and many others

Digital specification can also be of relevance to NFTs. Saving identifying and ownership data on blockchain will improve data integrity and privacy for many people. Parallel, quick and consistent transfers from these assets can eliminate global friction.

14.6 The story of Ethereum and CryptoKitties

CryptoKitties has been previously discussed, but its emergence is marvelous; hence, it is worth mentioning its relation with Ethereum.

Cryptokitties is an Ethereum-built game that enables players to collect, nurture and sell virtual cats, one of the first NFT initiatives to acquire popularity.

Each CryptoKitty has a unique combination of colour, breed and age. Also, they are not interchangeable. Cryptokitties tokens are indivisible, hence they cannot be split up (like the Ether for Gwei).

Cryptokitties gained prominence when clogged the block of blocks Ethereum due to heavy network activity. The all-time high (ATH) for daily transactions of Ethereum Blockchain remains about the popularity of the crypto cats. Like the first feather currency offering, other events also affected the Ethereum network (ICO).

Non-currency use cases for blocks date back to CryptoKitties. They generated millions in sales, with some rare artefacts commanding hundreds of thousands.

14.7 Detailed steps on how to create NFT art

Step 1: Create an artwork

The principal thing you should do to sell NFT craftsmanship is to make your specialty. This can be practically any type of media GIFs, representations, recordings, 3D models and so forth. A quick walk around Rarible or Foundation will give you a general idea of the crypto art inclinations.

At the moment, it seems to be a preference for either very avant-garde, experimental abstract art or meme-rich internet cultural references. Not that this should necessarily determine your work - we won't get into a debate about "making for the market" here. Once you've decided what art you'd like to upload, you can move on to the next step.

Step 2: Create an Ethereum wallet

There are numerous wallets to browse to serve your public location and store your private key, however it is by and large prescribed to depend on an equipment wallet.

If you're new to cryptocurrencies, here's a quick crash course on how cryptocurrency wallets work: Basically, they're software or hardware that help you manage the public address on your cryptocurrency blockchain.

This public address stores the cryptocurrency and can be seen by anyone, although its ownership is completely anonymous (unless you make it otherwise). Each public address has a private key which is used to deposit, withdraw or send funds to and from that address. Think of it as a mailbox: everyone sees it, knows where it is, and can send mail to it. However, only the people with the mailbox key can open it and collect the letters it contains.

There are two types of wallets: online wallets, which provide more convenience for the user at the expense of less security, and cold wallets, which store information offline and are less convenient for frequent use but provide a much higher level of security for the user.

A famous example of a hot wallet is the widely used MyEtherWallet, while the best examples of cold wallets are the hardware wallets from Trezor or Ledger that we mentioned above, as well as pen and paper. Yes, good old pen and paper can also work as a cold wallet, although you will need to create your own public addresses, which can be unpleasant.

Step 3: Buy ether

In the whirlwind of news and growing interest in the NFT, it may be news to you that selling the NFT will actually cost you some money. Unlike Bitcoin, where miners are rewarded with Bitcoin for contributing the computing power needed to verify transactions and add records to the blockchain, Ethereum miners are paid in another blockchain currency called gas.

Each time a transaction is requested to be confirmed and added to the blockchain, a transaction fee is paid (presumably to cover the gas and platform fee) - Ethereum miners can choose which contracts they would like to allocate computing power to, so the more gas you pay for your transaction, the quicker your contract will be executed and added to the blockchain. This includes uploading your NFT.

Step 4: Select a marketplace

Once you have your piece, your wallet and some ether burning a hole in your pocket, you are ready to put your NFT on the market. What you want to do is go to ethereum.org and take a look at their selection of "Apps" - short for decentralized apps. Rarible, Nifty Gateway and Foundation are amazing good opening points to get started to get familiar with the Ethereum market and see your NFT.

Each one caters to slightly different tastes, so be sure to check out all three, as well as many other marketplaces before settling on one.

Foundation seems to be best suited to digital painting, Nifty Gateway caters most to 3D models, and Rarible looks like a chaotic fusion of the aforementioned avant-garde and internet meme culture.

Step 5: Upload your artwork

While each principles will differ in where you press the actual button, they all start with connecting your cryptocurrency wallet. Each of the main sites will automatically create an account linked to your wallet and guide you through a fairly simple upload process, during which you will need to choose how many "copies" of the NFT you want to mint and what percentage of royalties you would like to receive once the product is resold.

The latter feature is an innovative step forward for digital artists who, unlike their traditional counterparts, have never been able to truly restrict the supply of any one work once it has been distributed and create a true "original".

The NFT essentially has a certificate of authenticity printed on the blockchain that proves that it is an original work, so that the original artist can get a cut of every subsequent trade/sale - a feature that even traditional artists cannot take advantage of. Once you have chosen your work, made your copies and set your royalties, you can move on to the final step.

Step 6: Pay the transaction fee

Once your NFT artwork has been locked and uploaded, all you have to do is pull the trigger and you can sit back and relax until your artwork is transferred to the blockchain and turns into an extraordinary substance on the organization, unchanging and impenetrable to any worker crash. The exchange expense will guarantee that your NFT is mined by any Ethereum digger who acknowledges the agreement and recuperates your charge for their work.

After that, your newly mined NFT should only be a matter of a couple of minutes before it hits the market, just waiting to delight the keen-eyed patron who sees it first.

15 NON-FUNGIBLE TOKEN MARKET

So far, NFTs have proven to be stable, and with all its use cases, it has gained more market place. Some of these market places have been discussed in the earlier chapters; it is time to discuss the step by step procedure on how to transact in some of these market places.

The crypto space has been fostering a new groundswell of institutional interest in the crypto industry for some time now. The newest company to invest in bitcoin is Tesla, the electric vehicle manufacturer. It also explains how to take an asset as payment in the future. This was a new development since it was owing to a discussion between Elon Musk and Michael Saylor, a wealthy tech entrepreneur, who bought bitcoin in 2020.

Tesla's announcement created a wave of enthusiasm among the crypto community.

While there is certainly a strong likelihood that loaded hedge funds would imitate the investing strategies of Tesla, Mass Mutual, Microstrategy, top digital funds, and inquisitive digital investors are seeking to identify the next big cryptocurrency investment opportunity (alts).

Divided Opinion on NFTs

New Financing Techniques are growing the digital resource market; meanwhile, the future of collectibles (in which digital tokens reflect ownership of either real or virtual items) is the means for users to verify their ownership by creating unique digital tokens stored on the blockchain. However, unlike crypto assets, the community has noted doubts about the real-world volume NFTs would drive. On the other hand, over 500 billion dollars' worth of weekly BTC futures trading volume took place in January of this year, and as of the time of this writing, NFT market trading volume has reached $8.2 million.

To far, NFTs such as digital paintings have failed to attract a strong trading market. However, with the sector maturing, it's possible that larger and more stable markets may develop. Of course, bringing in investors such as Paul Tudor Jones, Saylor and Musk is no different from previously having considered them mythical in cryptocurrencies.

With other items, you should be able to deposit your money on a blockchain and own collateralized fiat-pegged stable coins or borderless digital assets.

It's unclear if NFTs will be able to stay in the same slipstream as other cryptocurrencies like bitcoin and altcoins, and yet yield a profit. This is very important because is it able to make ordinary investors who spend small amounts of money in high-end auction houses and the preserve of high-net-worth collectors accessible to them?

Celebrities and NFTs

Already, Lindsay Lohan has started luring Bitcoin followers to her Twitter account, and billionaire Mark Cuban recently sold NFTs for about $1,000 to investors interested in selling his tweets as an NFT. Soon, other celebrities will jump on the bandwagon, and it will only be a matter of time before more elites join the movement.

In other words, Ethernity is trying to get famous individuals on board by selling digital artwork (including the aforementioned personalities) with every NFT. Paolo Maldini, Michael Rubin, and the Winklevoss twins will bless the collection. Michael Rubin is the creator of the All in Challenge, a charity campaign that has collected over $50 million to assist groups combating food poverty.

Nick Rose Ntertsas is the founder of Ethernity. Its website states that it is a platform for worldwide stars—celebrities, sportsmen, and artists—to endorse limited-edition artworks, and the money made from these sales will be donated to the star's chosen charity. Rose states that the artwork they have acquired is complete and ready for sale.

An example of recent success in using NFTs is Hashmasks. There is a venture in which digital portraits coexist with collectable NFTs, the appearance of which is both desired and highly sought. They have reached the $10M ETH mark in only a few days.

A unique and ultra-rare CryptoPunk NFT sold in ETH for $762,000. The digital art market cap is projected to surpass the market value of physical art, as digital art continues to grow.

Growing

According to Jehan, NFTs are the main missing link between physical and online publications.

NFTs are transparent and rare. This is because they are recorded in a public ledger, which protects valuable collectibles NFTs may play a key role in the decentralised finance (Defi) industry, according to some. Alpaca City's Ethereum-based virtual environment offers proof of concept for this.

Alpaca City's November token pre-sale raised over 1,000 ETH in 15 minutes. Owners can "breed" Alpaca NFTs, which will revolutionise the NFT market: NFT loans, interest-bearing accounts, etc. Interoperability is also required since NFT holders wish to send and receive assets from many blockchains.

Tracing and transferring tokens is now possible because to TRON's new NFT standard, TRC-721, which has a defi primitive. All of the stakeholders, both those in favor of NFTs and those opposed to them, are beginning to understand the true worth of NFTs. Secure and accessible NFT protocols are being offered by the companies, while purchasers race to acquire skin in the game. Decentralized Smart Contract Network Decentraland, Hashmasks, and CryptoPunks are all using Ethereum to launch NFT initiatives. Virtual reality is a world similar to a digital land, in which players may connect with others, explore, purchase land plots, and even establish new businesses.

Next Move?

Much will rely on investor interests, the VR/AR game industry's growth and profitability, and the introduction of

NFT-specific blockchains to power ecosystems. Finally, assuming gas costs stay constant, it is challenging to estimate NFT market potential (particularly Ethereum). Novel Financing Techniques have yet to show their capacity to maintain value over time, which is why important concerns won't go away for the time being. liquidity of NFTs is lower than that of more liquid financial instruments (but growing). It is quite simple to get one; but, finding a willing buyer who shares your own tastes is difficult.

People aren't excited about having unwelcome NFTs towards the end of the song when they can't play anymore. And right now, the celebration is in full flow. On February 8, a customer bought 9 separate NFT plots for $1.5 million. This transaction, too, set a new NFT record.

Digital real estate has now officially surpassed traditional real estate in price. It may be hysteria, but a growing number of crypto-savvy investors are running with the bulls.

What digitalists have discovered is that selling anything in the cyber realm may amplify the collective power of the public. All of humanity is connected, yet it is likely that tokenization will occur in the near future.

15.1 Selling an NFT

A simple guideline will work for all platforms, therefore it's a good idea to start with that guidance.

Setting your wallet

Before you can use cryptocurrencies or non-fungible tokens (NFTs), you will need a digital wallet to hold them. To further secure your transactions, we suggest that you use Google Chrome and install the MetaMask wallet plugin. Use this link to search for the commonly asked questions and suggestions for MetaMask. After you've installed OpenSea, go to the upper-right corner, click the icon, and then select My Profile. The instructions for logging in will be sent after you have your wallet.

Creating a collection

The page where you can view your account balance should be up now, however we are still working on it. Select My Collections, then click Create in the top-right corner. Once you have finished building your collection, name it and add a short description and a picture; we aren't establishing an NFT just yet; you will be able to modify all of this information once you've created your collection. Clicking the Add New Items button will take you behind the scenes and show you what your collection really is.

Fine-tuning your collection

While it's important to get started on the creation of your initial NFTs, there are a few things you should accomplish first. There is a customized banner to the right of the picture, seen above. Click on the "Make Your Own" pencil symbol in the top-right corner to submit your own logo. Aim for a size of about 1400x400, and avoid text. If you look at the Payments page, you will see pending secondary sales payments (which are now going to wait in your bank account) and selecting Visit will take you to the public collection.

Click "Edit" to add social links, images, and change the item's title, description, and picture. Additionally, if you keep the Accepted Payment Tokens option as it is, you will also have the option to set the resale tax up to 10%. If you wish to get 5% of the total sales price for your NFTs (for example), go to the "Receive a Percentage of Future Sales" page and put 5 in the "Commission to Recipients" box. Then, go to the page that says "Sellers Address" and enter your wallet address there. When you're completely satisfied, press the Submit Changes button and you will be sent to your company's back office.

Creating an NFT

The first NFT you'll make is under the Add new item heading. You will find an upload option to photos, videos, and audio files on the following page. In addition, you may name your NFT after selecting the choice from the drop-down menu. The process for adding an external link and a short description is finished next.

The NFT feature is currently limited to one instance at a time, therefore you will have to make several copies of a work and decide whether or not to include the edition number in the statistics area.

The advice provided previously was to make an individual token and then log into the insights to find the authorization number. In the event that you need to make more than one duplicate of a similar work (token ID), rather with multiple tokens and finding the authorization number in the insights, you can add ?enable supply=true to the end of the URL on the peak of the page and press Enter to reload. In order to modify the supply field, you need have completed this step first.

Keep in mind that you'll have to construct 100 individual sales lists (each with the amount set to "1") if you change the supply to, for example, 100.

At this time, it isn't feasible to have suppliers make 100 individual deals, and allow customers to select the amount of they would want to buy. Until this changes, it is not possible to modify the stockpile in the creation process.

Adding properties and levels helps streamline the exploration of your work by making it easier for collectors to locate your pieces. For example, "Year of creation" could be property of "2021".

Add unlocked material that only the owner of the item may see. Higher quality files, contact information for actual objects and access keys are all examples of unlocked material.

Once you have obtained a sense of contentment, click the Create button and fill in the message in your wallet. You wil not have to pay any petrol taxes to create an NFT (transaction costs). You'll see that your first NFT is neatly positioned beneath your search bar after you click the "Create" button. Click the pencil icon in the top-right corner of each NFT to alter it.

Announcement of items for sale

The easiest way to upload your NFT is to visit a publicly available property page and click on "Sell" (you can access it via your account page or by clicking on the property in the search bar you see above). Instead of a price-based auction, choose a fixed-price advertisement. When you are in a good mood, follow the directions in your wallet and then click on Publish your ad.

You will need to pay a petrol tax before you can list on OpenSea if you have never sold it before. Once the Ethereum blockchain becomes less congested, the trade should be simple. You will also be requested to verify the token in a non-ETH currency, which will incur a different (but lower) gas cost. So you won't have to pay anything the second time around.

If you accept a bid for an unlisted item using WETH, you will be requested to verify the WETH and pay a gas charge to accept the offer. When buying fixed-price listings, buyers pay a gas charge. When selling, sellers pay when accepting bids.

Since there are a lot of other users, don't be concerned if the transaction takes a little time to complete. When you return to re-enter the posting process, our framework will know that your wallet has completed the exchange and won't prompt you to pay costs when you set up the next posting.

15.2 Step-by-step procedure to sell an NFT in OpenSea.com

1. Download Metamask (https://metamask.io/) and install it. It is a Google Chrome extension.

2. Create a portfolio on Metamask. The following images are in Italian, but it easy to understand what is the right choice in English: start, create the wallet, I agree, create a password.

METAMASK

Aiutaci a Migliorare MetaMask

MetaMask vorrebbe raccogliere dati di utilizzo per capire meglio come gli utenti interagiscono con l'estensione. Questi dati verranno usati continuamente per migliorare l'usabilità e l'esperienza utente dei nostri prodotti e dell'ecosistema Ethereum.

MetaMask..

✓ Ti consentirà sempre di rimuovere il consenso tramite Impostazioni

✓ Invierà click e visualizzazioni di pagina in modo anonimo

✗ **Non** raccoglierà chiavi, indirizzi, transazioni, bilanci, hash, o qualsiasi altra informazione personale

✗ **Non** raccoglierà il tuo indirizzo IP completo

✗ **Non** venderà i tuoi dati per profitto. Mai!

No Grazie	Acconsento

Questi dati sono aggregati e sono quindi anonimi per le finalità del Regolamento generale sulla protezione dei dati (UE) 2016/679. Per maggiori informazioni sulla nostra politica sulla privacy, vedi Politica Privacy qua.

METAMASK

< Back

Crea Password

Nuova Password (minimo 8 caratteri)

Conferma Password

☐ Ho letto e accetto i Termini di Uso

Here is the view of Metamask by pressing on the Chrome extension.

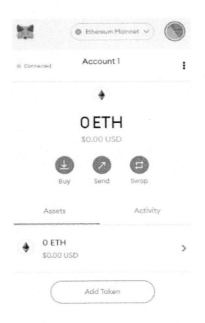

3. Move 0.1 ETH from your crypto wallet to your Metamask wallet.

This amount of Ethereum is necessary to validate the upload of your first item in your account).

It can vary due to the congestion of the blockchain.

If you do not have a crypto wallet, you can press "buy" in Metamask and buy your ETH here.

4. Go to Opensea.com, log in with your Metamask wallet, and create a Create/My collections collection.

The following image is an example:

5. Create an Item:

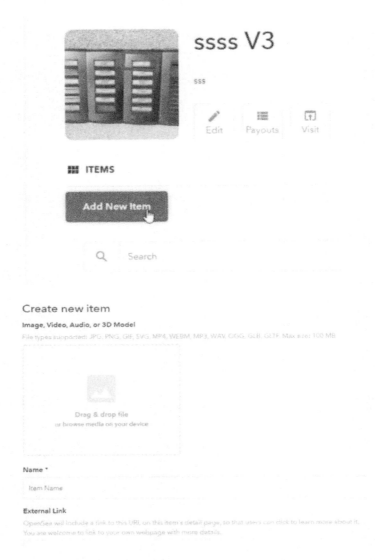

The following features are optional and depend on the type of NFT you are going to upload.

It is important to leave the number "1" because the item is

unique and therefore NOT FUNCTIONABLE.

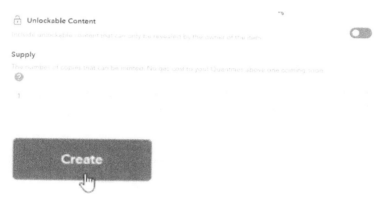

6. Sell your NFT

It is possible to choose a fixed price, put it on auction or bundle it.

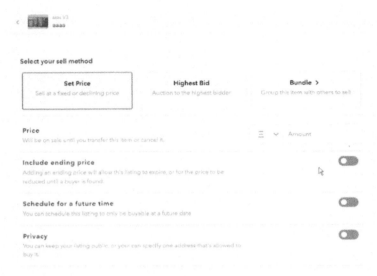

In the auction, we have to set the price. The minimum for sale is 1 ETH. We also need to set the end date of the auction.

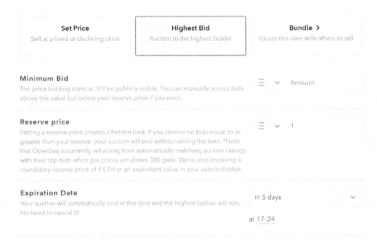

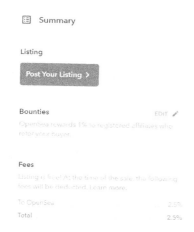

Listing

Post Your Listing >

Bounties   EDIT ✏

OpenSea rewards 1% to registered affiliates who
refer your buyer.

Fees

Listing is free! At the time of the sale, the following
fees will be deducted. Learn more.

To OpenSea   2.5%
Total   2.5%

7. Press "Post Your Listing" and pay the gas fees in ETH (around 0.1 ETH). These fees fluctuate a lot as it depends on how congested the Ethereum blockchain is.

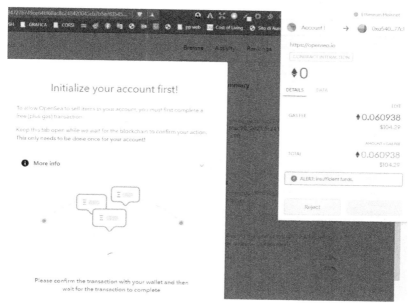

8. Sign with your Metamask Wall, and your NFT will be on sale.

15.3 Step-by-step procedure to sell an NFT in Rarible.com

As discussed earlier on how to create a Metamask wallet, you will also need a Metamask wallet to sell on Rarible website (https://rarible.com/).

1. Create your crypto wallet with Metamask: https://metamask.io/

2. Go to https://rarible.com/ and create an account. After creating an account, click in "Connect wallet"

3. Click in "Metamask" tab and sign in to your wallet. It's necessary to have at least 13 years old.

4. Click in "Create" and select the collectible type that you want create

5. Fill the form with the details of your NFT and click in "Create item"

6. Pay the gas fees and your NFT will be on sale

15.4 Step-by-step procedure to sell an NFT in NFTshowroom.com

- Go to https://hiveonboard.com/ and click "create an account"

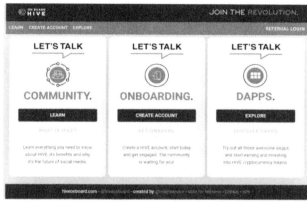

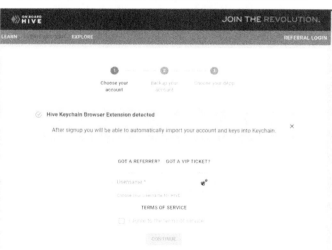

- Click in download backup, click in the blank box and then in "create hive account".

- Download and install the chrome extension of Hive Keychain:https://chrome.google.com/webstore/detail/hive-keychain/jcacnejopjdphbnjgfaaobbfafkihpep?hl=it

- Click the extension and then click in use keys/pwd and enter the data from the username and password in the file downloaded in hive on board.

```
Username: aaad
Password: Qycvja1dr7bUzrBHM7K66m6wvXYUr49s
```

Now your account is active.

- Now you have to buy HIVE coin. You have two possibilities:

- Buy in an exchange market, like Binance (https://accounts.binance.com/it/register?ref=52159529) and then move in your hive wallet.

- Buy directly with a credit card https://www.moonpay.com/ . This solution is a little bit more expensive than the first one.

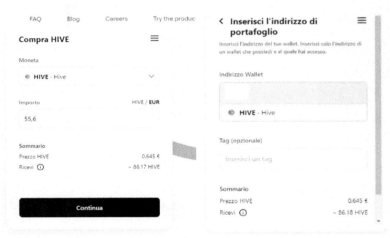

- Go to https://nftshowroom.com/ and login by entering your Hive wallet username, clicking in "Login with Keychain," and Hive wallet password.

- Click on your username and complete the profile's info. It's necessary to fill every field to be approved from this marketplace because the approval is manual and the team will check that you already have at least 5 images/videos in your website (you can create it for free with www.sites.google.com/new) or portfolio (7 days trial with www.portfolio.adobe.com) or Google Drive open link.

- Click apply to whitelist and wait 5-7 days (https://www.notion.so/NFT-Showroom-artist-guide-FAQ-and-whitelisting-3551e5437e0b443cb040a833750f6acb). The NFT Showroom teams will contact you in direct message in Instagram to validate your account. If you don't have an Instagram account, you have to create it. There isn't any other solution.

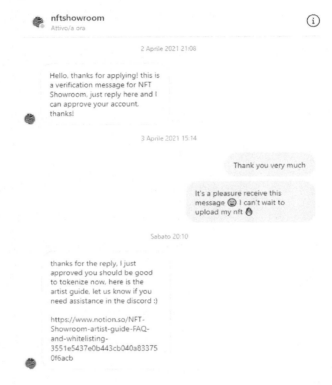

- After your account has been approved, you can start to upload your first NFT, going in nftshowroom, login in and click in "Tokenize".

- Choose what type of art you want upload; it's necessary a light version less than 1 Mb as a thumbnail and the normal size file of a maximum 30Mb.

- Complete every field. Mark NSFW (not safe for work) only if you upload inappropriate content.

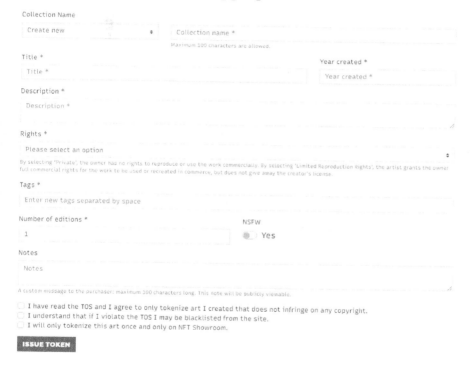

- Approve the uploading paying the 5 HIVE fee for the first NFT + 1 HIVE for every duplicate.

- Then wait for someone to buy your NFT.

16 TOOLS TO CREATE NFT FROM AN IMAGE

16.1 Goart Fotor

http://goart.fotor.com.s3-website-us-west-2.amazonaws.com/

16.2 Wordart

https://wordart.com/create

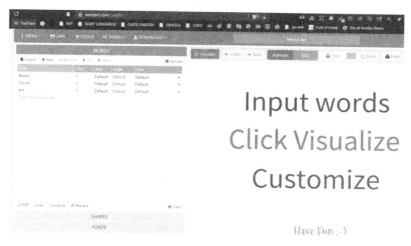

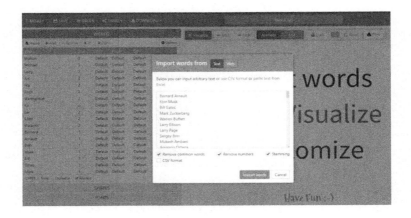

16.3 Night Café

Create Something Amazing

Show advanced options

New Feature: Bulk Create
Try your input image with multiple styles. Show advanced options, then "Try multiple styles".

Input Image
Choose an image to apply styles to

CHOOSE AN IMAGE

Style Image
Choose a style to apply to your input

CHOOSE A STYLE

Creation Settings

Input Image

Image Source
Preset: Image uploaded by user

Colour Settings
Using colours from the style images

Resolution
Low

Fidelity
55%

Smoothing
0%

Style 1 Image

Style 1 Source
Preset: Starry Night

Style 1 Weight
43%

Style 1 Mask
No mask applied

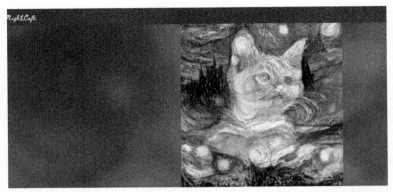

Untitled Creation ✎

Created 4 minutes ago

This creation is private. Make it public.

✎ 1 Style 🖼 Low Res

This artwork was created with the help of Artificial Intelligence. Create your
own AI-generated artwork using NightCafe Creator.

BUY A PRINT

DOWNLOAD

DUPLICATE

NEW CREATION

17 COMMON QUESTIONS WE GET ASKED IN CONSULTING.

This chapter summarizes the most common questions people have about NFTs.

Some of the topics covered in this portion of the Q&A have already been discussed in previous chapters; however, a review helps connect the information learned.

17.1 How do NFTs work?

These can be created on Blockchain contracts that support non-fungible tokens. NEO, EOS, and Ethereum were the first extensively used. Now also has a standard NFT-tokens, or NFT is a unique crypto asset that can be used to represent tangible and intangible goods. Real products are physical objects that can be touched, such as buildings, gadgets, etc., while intangible products can only be felt indirectly. Fungibility is the ability of assets that will be exchanged for the same items such as gold, dollars, etc. Non-fungibility is an irreplaceable or unique asset capability for art, etc.

Non-fungible tokens are a digital proof of authenticity and trustworthiness known as the blockchain. It keeps your transaction history record. NFT opens a creative platform for the items that are underestimated and provides collectors with easy ways to gather art digitally. Non-fungible tokens (NFTs) evolved with time and industry growth. Beeple is a popular name that appears in the world of NFTs.

NFTS can be created and issued in a variety of ways. For example, ERC-721, the Ethereum blockchain's standard for posting and trading non-fungible assets.

ERC-1155 is a newer standard. Tokens can be loaded into one contract, opening up additional possibilities. Interoperability is improved by standardising NFTS issuing. So assets may be moved between platforms very quickly.

If you want to save money while still admiring your NFTS choose a reputable wallet. Your NFT will be at the address. Notably, NFTs cannot be duplicated or transferred without the owner's authorization.

NFT can be traded on the OpenSea. They connect sellers and buyers, with each token having its own worth. Naturally, NFT prices fluctuate based on market supply and demand.

But how is that valuable? As with all valuable goods, the value is assigned by those who value it. The value is mutual trust. People believe in the value of fiat money, precious metals, and vehicles. Every valuable thing gains value the same way, so why isn't it stored digitally? Money does not exist for the purpose of having an exchange value. People think that money has worth regardless of whether it is fiat money, precious metals, or automobiles. In the same way, precious items everywhere rise in value, and that's why a digital library doesn't exist.

17.2 Where to Buy Digital Art

There is probably no better indication that anything is happening than a lack of knowledge and frustration, as well as specific inquiries and readily available responses. Until recently, the majority of high-priced art was purchased through a gallery, a trade show, or an auction house, ideally after viewing the item in its original form.

Consider how eloquently online viewing rooms are being deconstructed by galleries and trade fairs as a step in the wrong direction, as a substandard replacement for trade fairs that will be unable to take place during the outbreak of the epidemic. All of a sudden, people are buying artwork in the name of anonymity on online marketplaces that have no connection to the art sector, and in many cases, do not even have permission to serve the traditional art audience.

Contrary to this, even the largest and most popular markets, even those with auction records that are increasingly being read, rely on the followers of digital artists and new media artists to generate revenue. For example, if you scroll through the drops on Nifty Gateway, it quickly becomes apparent that the artists featured here are clearly chosen depending on the number of followers they have amassed.

The followers become collectors, and the art is dropped like sneakers and hoodies; there are unique items and open collections. Most of the time, the artists drop unique items and open collections; this is how the high sales sums come about. Open collection means that the art can be bought within a certain time window, five minutes, seven minutes, nine minutes; the number of sales is then the edition's size. The price per available collection is usually between $ 550 and $ 990. More than 100 works per edition are sold for $ 990. And that adds up.

Every day, there are drops on Nifty Gateway, the site launched by the twins Griffin Cock Foster and Duncan (name jokes have already been made), which are publicised in the platform's newsletter. Afterwards, it states: "TONIGHT'S drop will be available in 15 minutes!"

A few days ago, the server crashed during a drop because there was a lot of traffic. Of course, you can dismiss this as a sophisticated marketing strategy, complain about the loss of quality and say that none of this is art. And what is Christie doing with the Beeple NFT? Should the people who got incredibly rich with Bitcoin and Ether really get into art and shop at Christie's?

Kenny Schachter, the "Artnet" columnist, collector, gallery owner, curator, and artist, says in interviews and on Clubhouse time and again about digital art in the marketplaces that they are all just screensavers, gifs, and video game stills. "Like object on the back of a van," he said in an interview with "The Art Newspaper." Ne, like something from the internet that is now being sold on the internet. And the internet is full of memes and gifs, animations and renderings that relate to the context in which they are created.

At Clubhouse, it is explained by artists and experts like Lady Pheonix: "Bad art is what people collect and enjoy." And: "Memes are going to".

17.3 What does an NFT look like?

You can't touch NFTs because pretty much anything digital can be an NFT - a painting, music, videos, or even a cat GIF. A few days ago, the auction house Christie's sold the work Every day: The First 5000 Days by Mike Winkelmann, aka Beeple, for almost 70 million dollars. He posted a picture every day for 5000 days - now he has put them all together into one digital work. The buyer now receives the image file and an associated non fungible token. The proceeds catapult Winkelmann into the top 3 of the best-paid artists still alive. And that with a digital work of art that can never hang on a wall. The band Kings of Leon is releasing their new album When You See Yourself as NFT. Six of the NFTs will have a golden ticket that will give you front-row seats at the concerts for the rest of your life. Art activists bought a picture of Banksy, digitized it, and then burned it. This image is now only available in digital form as NFT; it will be auctioned on the OpenSea site.

OpenSea is the eBay of the NFTs, and it is very successful. In February, the platform had sales of $ 86.3 million, up from $ 8 million in January. Other sites that offer auctions include Rarible and Nifty Gateway. If you are interested in the Kings as mentioned earlier of Leon album or one of the Golden Tickets, you have to be able to dig deep into your digital pocket. FynnKliemann is also experimenting with NFTs. He auctioned 100 jingles for 250,000 euros.

Once again, people and organizations that can afford such experiments are in the lead. Investor Mark Cuban is one of them. Also, the NBA basketball league and FC Bayern Munich. The fantasy football platform Sorare can be described as a digital Panini album. The tickets of the individual footballers are extremely limited.

The enormous increase in value. The most expensive trading card so far was that of the player Mbappé from Paris Saint-Germain. It changed hands for $ 57,000. Because the card is registered via the blockchain, it cannot be counterfeited.

17.4 After Cryptocurrency comes to the crypto art

Crypto art is the new catchphrase that haunts the media landscape. There's a lot of this "art" on OpenSea. This digital art can still be duplicated, copied, and distributed, including NFTs. You don't have the image rights. NFTs only have one thing that cannot be copied: ownership of the work. Artists continue to retain all rights to the work, just like a real painting. As with art, anyone can buy a Banksy poster - but you can only own the original once.

17.5 What is the point and purpose of NFTs?

For artists, it is an opportunity to see money for the work and the work finally. Likes on Instagram are all well and good, but you don't earn anything with them. The artist can receive a percentage share in a resale of the NFT. FynnKliemann's jingles bring him ten percent of every resale. As a buyer, you see it more as an opportunity to appreciate digital art, much like a museum honors physical art. In any case, it is an investment that should pay off at some point.

17.6 There is also criticism of the hype.

NFTs are climate killers. A brief technical digression is necessary to explain this. The Ethereumblockchain, on which NFTs are based, uses a mechanism called Proof of Work. In so-called mining, the computer solves complex puzzles to be allowed to add new blocks to the blockchain. The difficulty of these tasks is artificially increased in order to prevent too much 'money from being generated too quickly. So, there is an arms race. Faster computers solve the puzzles in less time, new puzzles slow down the computers, so more computing power is needed, which in turn is slowed down with more difficult tasks. It should be clear that this principle hardly wins any sustainability award.

17.7 Are NFTs still worth it?

Suppose you have the necessary Cryptocurrency: of course. It is a business where supply and demand determine. The crypto objects can be bought and potentially profitably resold, just like classic art. Or maybe not. Every art market fluctuates; the market for crypto art is no different. Nobody can say when the hype will end.

17.8 Crypto Hype: What Are NFTs Anyway?

Before we get into NFT, we should briefly recap what a blockchain is so that it can be seen how non-fungible tokens fit in there. The most famous blockchain project is certainly Bitcoin. However, the Bitcoin blockchain is limited to use as a cryptocurrency platform. This is not the case with all blockchains.

This is how data storage works in the blockchain.

In general, a blockchain is a kind of database made up of blocks that are strung together like pearls on a chain. On the one hand, each block contains the actual data that is to be stored in it and, on the other hand, a unique hash value that ensures that the data content is unchanged.

In addition to its own hash value, each block on the chain knows the previous block's hash value. In this way, the blockchain authenticates itself in a kind of chain reaction. If a hash was changed anywhere in the chain, the chain would break.

In this way, the data in the blockchain is more secure from manipulation than in ordinary databases. The so-called NFT makes use of this aspect.

Non-fungible tokens

The term token is most closely linked to its use as an asset. A token can also represent an asset or an economic good or be a digital equivalent of a real good.

In relation to a cryptocurrency, all tokens are fungible, i.e., interchangeable. This means that each token represents an equal asset; it does not matter what specific token you have. It is worth the same as any other holder's token. This is how our money works too. It doesn't matter which specific ten-euro note you use. You can also use two five-euro bills or five two-euro coins or any combination. The means, in this case, means of payment, are exchangeable.

This is precisely not the case with the NFT. Non-fungible, i.e., non-exchangeable tokens, represent a very specific asset and are therefore unique. They only have the technology of storage on the blockchain in common with currency tokens.

This makes NFT ideal for assets of which there are only one or a few. These are currently digital trading cards, game characters, virtual stretches of land in virtual worlds, or so-called crypto art. However, identity cards, vaccination cards, or other important documents could also be stored and secured via the blockchain.

Crypto collectibles and NFT art as dominant use cases - currently.

The most important or at least widespread use cases of NFT at the moment are crypto art and digital collectibles. Let's start with the collectibles.

Anyone who has ever played Magic the Gathering or Yu-Gi-Oh or Pokémon with real cards knows that success lies in owning the right cards. There is also a collector's aspect, i.e., the desire to own particularly rare or popular cards. So, a market has developed in which individual cards are sold for thousands of euros.

With NFT, this model can be transferred to the blockchain. A car manufacturer would create 20 copies of a particular trading card as a digital asset and store it on the blockchain. Now 20 potential buyers could buy this asset and later prove their ownership.

Anyone who thinks that this is theoretical should take a look at OpenSea - one of the largest of the now quite numerous marketplaces for NFT. OpenSea contains all kinds of collectibles and digital art objects or assets that can be used in virtual worlds such as Decentraland.

In early March 2021, BTC Echo reported the sale of a virtual area in the collectible monster game Axie Infinity for 1.5 million US dollars, or around 890 ethers, the Cryptocurrency on the Ethereum platform. This transaction replaced the previous record holder, the Cryptokitties Dragon, for what is probably the most famous blockchain game Cryptokitties. The kitten, which looks more like a hamster with a dinosaur tail, changed hands for 600 ether.

More and more artists are also relying on NFT to sell digital works with a guarantee of uniqueness. The Canadian singer Grimes had made around six million dollars in sales within 20 minutes with an NFT sale on the Nifty Gateway platform. The

German artist FynnKliemann is currently auctioning 100 specially made jingles as NFT. Leon's band Kings is selling their new album "When You See Yourself" on Open Sea in a 14-day auction.

Twitter CEO Jack Dorsey also wants to participate in the NFT hype. A few days before the microblog platform's 15th birthday, Dorsey is auctioning an automatic copy of the Valuables website's first tweet. The current highest bid is $ 2.5 million.

11 projects build a strong foundation under the DEFI and NFTS marriage

Meet team makes the NFT market almost equally complex, flexible, and liquid as the rest of Crypto.

The digital collection on Blockchains moves retail mania for higher Crypto now, partly because they are cool and partly because the market seems to arrive at this consensus finally: the ownership of digital goods that can be proven can obtain rea merit.

When there is genuine merit, there is money to be made. Ir recent years, it has been demonstrated that this collection o tokens, also known as non-fungible (NFTS) tokens, has a very high value.

Currently, a new fund for NFTFI is being established as a data point in the storey of the union of NFTs and Decentralization Finance (DEFI). This technology enables borrowers to deposit digital things as collateral on their credit reports. Among those who contributed to the $ 890,000 round were RoehhamGhehamlou, Dapper Labs Coinfund, Lao,1kx and others. NFTFI announced the investment on Thursday.

NFTFI is one of various companies that make it more easier to obtain money, get results, and get money back from the digital collection room by partnering with third-party vendors.

How does it work?

Ave and Defi Giants Compound are basically similar in that they are both money markets, but they both use fungible guarantees, like various stable coins or ET, to operate. NFT is not viable, because they are markets with a lack of liquidity, which makes it more difficult to locate prices in these markets.

When more items are introduced to the market, it changes more quickly, making it easier for liquidity to flow through a greater number of creations. And keep in mind that this is Crypto: In our industry, rapid change means quite different things than it did in the old era of social networks and Pokey phones, which is a good thing.

Several press releases have said that "NFTs begin to conceptualise new financial service categories when they foresee how we establish and recognise digital content's ownership online," according to MitraLasse Clausen, a partner at 1kx venture capital business.

The following 10 initiatives, which are separate from NFTFI, function to almost similar extents to complicate, adapt, and liquidate the NFT market, as well as the rest of the Crypto space:

Nintex.

The startup, the platform, is working on a new edition with numerous additional features. The government over the underlying NFT is for holders of tools and fractions that allow more delicate ownership. A DAO will also run the entire app. "This is a no-brainer. Uniqueness reigns supreme "Joel Hubert told Coindesk in an email.

Ark Gallery.

As a result, NFT pioneer lava labs become more fungible. Ark then established additional mechanisms to increase liquidity for non-fungible original tokens, which may be credited for the current crypto punks boom. We're working on the blank. "We will start the NFT project," Roberto Ceria Ark told Coindesk in an email.

Mintbase.

Mintbase makes it easy to create non-fungible tokens. It recently had a Sino-led funding round. Mint base permits sales royalties to be distributed to up to 1,000 persons. COO CAROLIN told Coindesk, " "It's really a part of the fractional ownership discussed by everyone".

NFTX

This allows public index funds to own many NFTs with one token. It features tokens for NFT categories and the market spectrum. "Many people do not have the knowledge or time to trade individual NFTs but desire market exposure.

17.9 Defi

A hot new trend is well underway in the crypto community: Defi. Although Defi is not exactly new, the YFI crypto token's success has sparked new interest in Defi and its associated cryptocurrencies among traders and investors. Even if you are only trading the bigger cryptocurrencies like Bitcoin and Ethereum, it is worth keeping an eye on the Defi boom as it could be affecting your assets. Here is a brief guide to what is going on at Defi, YFI, and the wider crypto market.

Nice increase at YFI

Cryptocurrency prices have been in a superior advantage, as cryptocurrency stole the show from everyone else when its value rose 165% to $ 38,682. This token is YFI, the governance token for decentralized finance (Defi) of the yearn Finance platform.

Yearn aggregates the various yields through the Defi logs. The users generate income by lending their coins to various protocols or by storing them in "vaults." Governance tokens such as YFI can also be purchased by users who provide liquidity for the process known as "yield farming." As the name suggests, the holders of these governance tokens can also vote on the network's proposals.

YFI-like coins also jumped on the Defi bandwagon and reached higher prices. The price of YF Link rose to $ 581 (328%), that of YFFI to $ 84.14 (465%), and that of YFV to $ 56.62 (201%). YFII, an offshoot of YFI, rose from $ 935 to $ 5,076 in three days.

Governance tokens are becoming a popular speculative asset as their supply is limited, and investors want to get in before it is too late. The range of YFI tokens is limited to just 30,000 pieces, with 29,962 tokens already in circulation at the time this article was written. One of the reasons there are such dramatic price movements is because these tokens are highly liquid, and a single large transaction can have a huge impact on the price.

17.10 Invest in Defi

It seems like everyone wants to get into Defi, but what does this term actually mean? Defi stands for "Decentralized Finance" and aims to replicate our traditional financial system's application areas with high-tech and little bureaucracy and without intermediaries. This means that issuing and borrowing, trading derivatives and securities, taking out insurance, investing, etc., is all done through a decentralized open-source network rather than banks. Smart contracts, which the participants in the blockchain verify, automatically execute the terms of the financial agreements. Defi smart contracts are currently valued at roughly USD$8 billion.

Defi and Ethereum

This should sound familiar to anyone interested in Ethereum. In fact, the vast majority of these applications run on Ethereum. Other platforms with opportunities for smart contracts should work for Defi as well, but Ethereum is currently leading the field. In theory, DeFi's popularity should give ETH a healthy boost too.

Yearn Finance's core products are "safes" that offer yield farmers the best returns while pooling money to reduce users' workload. The crypto community already expects the upcoming launch of Yearn's ETH vaults to increase demand for ETH and decrease supply as more Ethereum tokens are locked in the vault for yield farming.

17.11 Boom or bubble?

While some investors are quick to jump at the chance of impressive returns that yield farming promises, following the latest trend is not always the right step. Long-time crypto enthusiasts will still remember the 2017-2018 ICO bubble well. Many Defi projects are still speculative and involve both risks and rewards.

Yield farming, which is really driving the Defi rush, has also been criticized by industry leaders.

Ethereum co-founder VitalikButerin has warned investors to be careful when it comes to Defi. He compares the business model of yield farming (which drives inflation in the supply of governance tokens) to the Federal Reserve's printing.

Invest in the crypto future with StormGain

As always, the savvy trader will do his research on particular investments. But as soon as the dust has settled concerning the Defi boom, Cryptocurrency will win across the board as the areas of application of the blockchain become more and more apparent. That is why we recommend a diverse and flexible crypto portfolio on a platform that offers you high rewards for your participation.

Stormin is the most effective cryptocurrency trading platform on the market. Stormin is available on the Internet or as a smartphone app and offers the opportunity to trade the top 6 cryptocurrencies with a leverage of up to 200x around the clock - on a user-friendly interface available in several languages. Stormin also offers the best customer bonuses on the market, including up to 15% annual interest on cryptocurrency deposits.

18 HOW AUCTIONING WORKS IN THE MARKETPLACE

NFTs are part of a $250 million industry that is rapidly growing.

According to a 2020 study by L'Atelier BNP Paribas, the market for non-fungible tokens, or NFTs, has grown to $250 million. As cryptocurrencies like Bitcoin continued to rise in popularity, investments in NFTs surged 299 percent in 2020.

NFT manufacturers and resellers made millions. After paying $67,000 for the Beeple project, an art collector made $6.6 million on a 10-second video artwork.

NFTs include digital trading games, virtual real estate, art, and cards. Here's how to buy and sell NFTs.

NFTs, unlike common cryptocurrencies such as Bitcoin and Ether, cannot be directly traded and distributed through a variety of platforms.

Most NFT platforms allow buyers to have a digital wallet and use Flow, WAX, or Ethereum.

Here's how to buy and sell NFTs.

For both designers and sellers, digital art has taken in millions of dollars.

On Nifty Gateway, "Crossroads" by Mike Winkelmann was resold for USD$6.6 million.

The majority of digital-art trading platforms allow artists to collect royalties. Some of them cater to a select few, while others encourage everyone to create and sell their work.

NFTs gave a windfall of benefit to professional digital artists. Digital-art trading platforms, according to NFT artist Trevor Jones, may prevent the need for more conventional art markets. NFTs have also attracted the attention of several traditional auction houses. Christie's, a 1766-founded auction house, auctioned a Beeple piece in February, marking the first foray into digital tokens. Currently, the painting is valued at $9.75 million, with two days left to go until the auction ends.

The work of multimillion-dollar digital artists may be found on platforms such as Nifty Gateway, Foundation, and SuperRare which allow purchasers to choose from a carefully curated collection of work.

It is great because Nifty Gateway allows artists who have only lived on Instagram and Twitter to showcase their work.

Following the adoption of crypto currency, they started selling crypto art and are now enjoying the benefits and growing fame.

On sites like Nifty Gateway, SuperRare, and Foundation, artists such as digital comic artist Chris Torres and Grimes have found homes. These websites compensate artists with a royalty of approximately 10% of any potential sales of their work.

The use of credit cards by buyers is intended to make Nifty Gateway's site more accessible to buyers, but other platforms lay a stronger emphasis on decreasing the entrance barrier for developers.

In contrast to Zora and Rarible, which are invite-only sites, Mintable and Rarible let anybody to publish, sell, and trade images and text as non-traditional assets.

Artists can still earn royalties on these pages, but the content is considerably less carefully regulated than on the other pages. Users of Rarible can submit anything they choose, from blank photographs to their own adaptations of well-known pieces of art.

Robert Martin, an NFT developer on Rarible, believes the sites need to strengthen their security, but he praises the ease with uploading content to Rarible.

These websites offer NFTs for sale at various prices from $10 to hundreds of thousands.

18.1 OpenSea

With everything from trading cards to sports, virtual reality and art, OpenSea bills itself as the world's largest non-financial-transaction (NFT) marketplace. On the internet, there are over 200 categories and 4 million things to choose from.

Ether can be used to purchase common NFT products such as CryptoPunks, CryptoKitties, and virtual real estate on OpenSea.

OpenSea is used by a number of marketplaces, including Decentraland, which is a popular virtual real-estate platform. The NFTs sold by OpenSea have generated approximately USD$24 million in revenue, according to DappRadar.

Opensea requires you to fill out a form on MetaMask as (https://opensea.io/).

18.2 NFT and sports

NBA Top Shot distributes sports footage for a variety of prices ranging from $20 to several thousand dollars.

The popularity of fantasy sports has also had an impact on NFT revenue. A unique fantasy soccer platform is available that allows users to create, sell and manage virtual clubs using digital player cards.

This site was launched in 2018, it has only just begun to acquire popularity among users. The cryptocurrency news site CryptoSlam reports that Sorare just sold almost USD$13 million in ether.

CryptoSlam requires you to fill out a form on MetaMask and Google (https://cryptoslam.io/)

18.3 Gamers and trading-card collectors

Axie Infinity produces NFTs for the gaming environment. Axie Infinity produces NFTs for the gaming environment. Axie Infinity is a fictional character created by Axie.

Axie requires you to fill out a form on google as (marketplace.axieinfinity.com/login?)

CryptoSlam says that Axie Infinity, a company that offers cartoon animals designed to fight in a Pokmon-like way, is one of the top ten most popular websites on the web for crypto-collecting.

The expansion of non-traditional gaming is projected to continue. Combat Racers, a blockchain racing game developed by Altitude Games, was released on the Arkane Market, which currently has over 100,000 players.

Myth is another famous trading card and memorabilia website. Market and Treasureland are two of my favorite places in the world. The growth of NFT gaming is expected to continue.

18.4 Virtual real estate market

On Decentraland, users may purchase and trade virtual real estate. Janine Yorio, who is the co-head of Republic Real Estate, foresees a role for digital real estate to emerge as the next major investment industry in Decentraland.

Using virtual reality and real estate, Decentraland, a non-fungible token (NFT) platform built on the Ethereum blockchain and owned and operated by individuals, makes use of the Ethereum blockchain. It's a multiplayer game to play roles, allowing players into a networked first person shooter to build a virtual world (NFT). According to Yorio, the game resembles a more advanced version of "SimCity," "Minecraft," or "Fortnite."

It has been reported that Atari, the firm that created Pacman, has ambitions to build a bitcoin casino on this platform.

The price of the platform currency named "MANA" has increased by more than 321 percent in the past 12 months and now this currency has a capitalization of $225 M.

Decentraland requires you to fill out a form on google as (https://market.decentraland.org/)

The site's very first tweet is auctioned off as a non-financial transaction, stated Twitter CEO Jack Dorsey (NFT). The digital asset now is 2.5 million dollars, depending on its market value Valuables is a platform that lets users to sell their tweets in exchange for ether, which is a cryptocurrency. The website is solely dedicated to the sale of tweets in the form of NFTs Another platform on trend is Glass Factory.

You can create digital art like holograms and sell them as tokens on the secondary market.

The artist Peter Rudwall sold his personal information as NFT, including his social media profiles, weight, and birth date

19 FUTURE OF NON-FUNGIBLE TOKENS

Since the inception of NFT, the popularity of NFT games has skyrocketed. As of January 2019, Dapper Labs, the company that created CryptoKitties, has begun collaborating with other NFT providers in order to facilitate interoperability between game platforms. This means that a native NFT from one platform can now be used on another platform without modification. NFT projects have been created by a number of major organisations, including the video game producer NBA and Ubisoft.

In recent years, the potential for NFTs has extended dramatically beyond the gaming industry. Organizations and organisations are investigating the potential of non-fungible tokens as a means of establishing identity as well as for certification, ticketing, and fractional ownership of both digital and physical assets. Any situation in which there is a requirement for traceability and clear ownership falls under the purview of NFT use cases.

The future of NFTs will heavily depend on the progress of the Ethereum network and wider blockchain technology.

185

It's safe to assume that as blockchain technology continues to grow, NFTs will follow – whether it's on the Ethereum blockchain, another public network, or a private network.

<u>Crowdfunding a non-fungible token</u>

Non-fungible tokens are still relatively new, and most game developers have had to figure out how they can be made as they go. This means that many NFTs are built using existing smart contracts or by creating their protocol. In some cases, the founders of an NFT will also create a game to showcase its features and utility. This allows users to purchase the game and give it a level of credibility.

19.1 The NFT Approach to Crowdfunding

Funding for a new company by using crowdfunding is a relatively new concept. NFTs (Non-Fungible Tokens) have been accessible on the Ethereum network since 2015. But among game creators and a broader audience, they are still relatively obscure. This means that many developers may not have the tools or resources to create an NFT. This is one of the reasons that the NFT Approach to Crowdfunding was created. This approach makes it possible for NFTs to be created, hosted, and distributed on any platform (including mobile devices and web browsers). In addition, game developers can also build their own crowdfunding campaign using the "NFT-Crowdfund" standard. It provides developers with the tools and resources they need to create their own NFT. This allows them to create their own ERC-721 token — which is an NFT that can be used as a crowdfunding campaign.

19.2 Creating NFT-Crowdfund

Here is how you can potentially build your own NFT-Crowdfund:

1) Create your colored token for crowdfunding on a platform (Ethereum Wallet, Metamask, etc.) or via a command-line interface (console).

2) Use NFT-Crowdfund protocol for creating and distributing the NFT.

3) Use ERC 721 to describe your game items.

4) Use ERC – 684 for creating pre-order items with a discount. These will not be fungible after the Crowdfund ends. Unsold pre-order items are burned.

5) List your rare item(s) on a marketplace for selling post-crowdfunding using the NFT registry, or create your own marketplace. Rename your NFT if needed to reflect the marketplace name. All pre-order items must be re-categorized to match your new marketplace category.

1) Create your colored token for crowdfunding on a platform (Ethereum Wallet, Metamask, etc.) or via a command-line interface (console).

2) Use NFT-Crowdfund protocol for creating and distributing the NFT.

3) Use ERC 721 to describe your game items.

19.3 Hype Art NFT Marketplace

Finally, I wanted to introduce you to this revolutionary project named Hype Art. I am developing with a team of art and cryptocurrency lovers.

Non-For-Profit (NFP) projects began to gain widespread notice. Although crypto was going through a downturn at the time, the industry saw significant growth because of it.

The most used marketplaces for NFT (Superrare, Niftigataway, Rarible) are presenting their platforms in a way that is more similar to Amazon and eBay than to an art gallery: collectors don't feel any artistic experience when browsing these platforms.

The artist is not at the center of the discussion. No space is given to the vision and the thought behind its work.

19.3.1 What do we want to create?

We think the artistic vision of the NFT creator needs to be placed at the center of the narrative. Each artist will be able to share the creative idea behind their work through a live interview (hosted by Koinsquare) together with a curated description of the work presented.

We aim to create a 3d virtual gallery that allows the collector to replicate the same feeling of seeing works displayed in a real gallery.

We want to stimulate the community of our collectors by using gamification; therefore, auctions will be made in parallel to airdrops to our followers.

19.3.2 Where?

Hype.art will use Opensea (ETH blockchain) and FAN (Tron blockchain) as platforms where the auction will take place, to access a bigger market.

Hype.art will instead provide the artistic promotion towards the community and a structured team to allow artists to customize their "online exhibitions".

19.3.3 Key players

There are 3 key players: Zulu Republic, Koinsquare and Satoshygallery.

The **Zulu Republic** is a place that exists on the blockchain where people, businesses, and organizations can thrive on their own terms. Our purpose is to help advance the development of decentralized technology, which is likely to have an enormous impact on the advancement of human rights and empowerment throughout the world, as well as the mitigation of the digital gap.

Koinsquare is a project that aims to promote and disseminate information and knowledge in the field of blockchain and cryptocurrency technology.

With our commitment, passion and professional approach, we present and analyze different topics such as Cryptocurrencies, Smart Contracts, centralized / decentralized Exchanges, ICOs, Fintech Industry, Market values of the major crypto assets, Mining systems and much more.

Sathoshy Gallery was born in a very early stage of cryptocurrency history. Since 2013, it is using iconography and art to fill the gap between technology developers and the general public and spread the crypto culture to a larger audience. Satoshigallery has provided art paintings to various private collectors worldwide, illustrated books for Andreas Antonopoulos, and drew some of the most iconic logos in the crypto space (Bitfinex, Tether, etc.).

19.3.4 When will the project launch?

- March 2021: Hype.art was born

- April 2021: Platform and artistic development

- May 2021: Marketing development

- September 2021: Launch of platform for public

19.3.5 Do you want to partecipate to AirDrop?

Artist exhibition will include thousands of Airdrops and a premium Auction, ready to scream out the first Artist with the launch of Hype.art. You have been one of the first to get an invitation to view the Exhibition and to bid in the Auction. We will be providing a date announcement to the subscriber as soon as possible.

Subscribe to the newsletter to not miss any news: **www.hype.art**.

20 CONCLUSION

This book attempts to educate readers on non-fungible tokens, what they are, and how they can benefit businesses. It explores the details of the NFT marketplace and where its future is headed. We also touch on the myths that surround non-fungible tokens, as well as what you can do to create your own NFT. Hopefully, this book has helped you better understand non-fungible tokens and how they can be used in your business in the future.

- Please review my book here: http://www.amazon.com/review/create-review?&asin=B095M47KH4

- At the following link, you can access a **completely free online course** on "NFT Artist":
https://dl.bookfunnel.com/j699cthbam

21 REFERENCES

- *https://coinmarketcap.com/alexandria/article/what-is-a-non-fungible-token-nft?cv=1*
- *https://www.forbes.com/sites/lawrencewintermeyer/2021/02/12/non-fungible-token-market-booms-as-big-names-join-cryptos-newest-craze/?sh=57*
- *https://academy.binance.com/en/articles/a-guide-to-crypto-collectibles-and-non-fungible-tokens-nfts*
- *https://opensea.io/blog/digital-art/the-beginners-guide-to-creating-selling-digital-art-nfts/*
- *https://www.investopedia.com/non-fungible-tokens-nft-5115211*
- *https://www.maxfosterphotography.com/gallery/what-is-an-nft-how-can-photographers-and-artists-benefit/*
- *https://www.businessinsider.com/nft-marketplaces-where-to-buy-sell-non-fungible-tokens-online-2021-3?r=US&IR=T*
- *https://influencermarketinghub.com/nft-marketplaces/*
- *https://beincrypto.com/top-10-most-expensive-nft-sales-globally/?cv=1*
- *https://observer.com/2021/04/five-things-artists-should-know-and-do-before-getting-into-nfts/*
- *https://www.gemini.com/cryptopedia/nft-non-fungible-token-crypto-collectibles*
- *https://www.esquire.com/entertainment/a35742083/what-are-nfts-explained/*
- *https://cointelegraph.com/news/five-of-the-most-expensive-nfts-sold-in-2019*
- *https://petapixel.com/2021/03/12/what-is-an-nft-and-why-should-photographers-care/*

- *https://gadgets.ndtv.com/internet/news/nft-non-fungible-tokens-what-are-they-blockchain-cryptocurrency-assets-unique-digital-physical-2382693*
- *https://www.coindesk.com/how-to-create-buy-sell-nfts*
- *https://www.britannica.com/technology/photography/Into-the-21st-century-the-digital-age*
- *https://www.wibbitz.com/blog/infographic-video-production-evolution-timeline/*
- *https://www.nbcnews.com/think/opinion/what-are-nfts-what-could-they-do-music-industry-artists-ncna1261205*
- *https://news.slashdot.org/?issue=20210305*
- *https://pixelplex.io/blog/non-fungible-tokens/*
- *https://decrypt.co/resources/non-fungible-tokens-nfts-explained-guide-learn-blockchain*
- *https://art.art/wp-content/uploads/2021/03/NFT-YEARLY-REPORT-2020.pdf*
- *https://www.coinstaker.com/uk-government-storage-evidences-on-blockchain/*
- *https://www.businessinsider.co.za/nft-marketplaces-where-to-buy-sell-non-fungible-tokens-online-2021-3*
- *https://www.tandfonline.com/doi/abs/10.1080/03610910802680880*
- *https://forkast.news/nft-art-nba-top-shot-crypto-collectibles/*
- *https://tokenbank.co.kr/coin/310/view/*
- How Legal are Non-Fungible Tokens (NFTs) in Singapore .... https://singaporelegaladvice.com/legal-non-fungible-tokens-nfts-singapore/
- Non-Fungible Token Definition: Understanding NFTs. https://www.investopedia.com/non-fungible-tokens-nft-5115211

- How to Create an NFT Marketplace Platform? | by Linda John https://medium.com/the-capital/how-to-create-an-nft-marketplace-platform-b3dad5ae1ecc
- What are NFTs – and why is the whole art world talking .... https://vr-nft.com/what-are-nfts-and-why-is-the-whole-art-world-talking-about-them/
- An article from 'The New York Times', sold for 478,573 euros. https://newsrnd.com/tech/2021-03-26-an-article-from--the-new-york-times---sold-for-478-573-euros.HkJNgDoEu.html
- How to Make, Purchase, and Sell NFTs? – NFT Hours. https://nfthours.com/how-to-make-purchase-and-sell-nfts/
- NFTs: What Are They and How Can You Create Them?. https://techmepro.com/how-to/nfts-what-are-they-and-how-can-you-create-them/
- What makes NFTs go?. "Twitter CEO, Jack Dorsey sold his https://pdiwan.medium.com/what-makes-nfts-go-fcf07d3e3c6c
- Non-Fungible-Token Market Booms As Big Names Join Crypto's https://www.forbes.com/sites/lawrencewintermeyer/2021/02/12/non-fungible-token-market-booms-as-big-names-join-cryptos-newest-craze/
- 11 Projects at the Nexus of DeFi and NFTs - CoinDesk. https://www.coindesk.com/defi-nft-projects
- Top 5 Best NFT Marketplaces For Artists - NFT's Street. https://www.nftsstreet.com/best-nft-marketplaces-for-artists-2/

- Unreal Real Estate Makes Its Curious Debut. https://www.premierhomesearch.com/blog/487/Unreal+Real+Estate+Makes+Its+Curious+Debut
- Collinson Crowdfunding-Your Gateway to Innovative Investments. https://www.ccfl.co.nz/raising-capital/key-benefits

NON-FUNGIBLE TOKENS YEARLY REPORT 2020. https://observatorioblockchain.com/wp-content/uploads/2021/02/NFT-YEARLY-REPORT-2020-FREE-EN.pdf

22 THANKS

In this book, I have included all the knowledge, strategies and solutions I have learned about NFTS.

I hope you have enjoyed this publication, which took me months of work and sacrifices.

Thank you for reading this book; I admit it was not easy to make this publication. I hope it will be useful to you, and I would be happy to receive your opinion with an unbiased and honest review; it would mean a lot to me and help me improve in future publications.

Thank you very much. I hope to update the book soon with lots of new tips. I will look forward to your best suggestions.

Crypto Art AI

Printed in Great Britain
by Amazon